To Cliffie Stoodley

Compliments of John West

1- 16 - 84

The Money Workbook for Women

THE MONEY WORKBOOK FOR WOMEN

A STEP-BY-STEP GUIDE TO MANAGING YOUR PERSONAL FINANCES

Carole Phillips

ARBOR HOUSE · NEW YORK

Library of Congress Catalog Card Number: 81-71696

ISBN: 0-87795-379-1 (clothbound edition)
ISBN: 0-87795-402-X (Priam trade paperback)

Manufactured in the United States of America

Designed by Barbara Huntley

10   9   8   7   6   5   4   3   2   1

To Andrew and Elizabeth

ACKNOWLEDGMENTS

With much appreciation, I wish to thank:

my husband, Almarin Phillips, for sharing the joy and agony of writing and his ever cheerful willingness to serve as resident sounding board;

my assistant, Jacqueline Smith, whose abundant talents now can be liberated from typing endless drafts and checking the facts;

my friend, Alan Halpern, living proof that fairy godparents come in many different guises;

my agent, Mary Dolan, for her confidence and low key, but always sound, advice;

Arthur Baldadian, Bernard Bernstein, Ann Costello, Louise Gilbert, Robert LeClair, Harold Sampson, Nancy Smith and Thomas Weiner for sharing so generously their time and professional expertise;

and most of all, my father, Joseph Cherry, who taught me, among so many things, that being a woman and being "smart about money" are not mutually exclusive.

CONTENTS

PREFACE

On October 2, 1976, I organized one of the country's first Women and Money programs for my employer at that time, the Provident National Bank in Philadelphia. You would have thought, from the response to the program's announcement, that we had reinvented the credit card. Three hundred and fifty women signed up for the all-day event, and about twice that many were turned away.

The Economic Conference for Women, as we called it, was a valuable learning experience in many ways. The female professionals who led our workshops—on credit, investments, real estate, insurance, estate planning and tax planning—found themselves, as one put it, "feeling touched and privileged to be able to give something back to our own kind." Time and again throughout the day, women of all ages and income levels told us how grateful they were for a financial program tailored to the unique needs of women who could share information in an informal, supportive environment made up of "our own kind."

After that initial success, my colleagues and I were asked to run similar one-day workshops for college alumnae associations, church and synagogue groups, and other social, professional and civic organizations whose members are women. We were delighted to do it—to spread the word, so to speak—but we began to have mixed feelings about the long-term value of one-day stands. Yes, the workshops raised people's consciousness, perhaps motivated some of them to take a course in investing or read the financial page of the newspaper, but a one-day workshop was like going to a Chinese restaurant—all the food comes at once, you eat until you think you'll burst, and a few hours later you're hungry again.

The process of learning to make intelligent financial decisions required more than a "quick fix." But we weren't sure exactly what.

The answer came to me in the fall of 1979 when I was asked to take over the Women and Money course at Temple University's Division of Educational Services for Women and Men. I decided that rather than talk about investments, insurance and other financial matters as if they were unrelated phenomena, my course would consider each topic within the framework of an individual's total financial needs. Thus there was a unifying concept—the concept of financial planning—to provide week-to-week continuity and tie together the bits and pieces of personal money management.

Secondly, this would be a "do-it-yourself" workshop, with the accent on *work*. Assignments were structured so that students had to apply our class discussions to their own financial situations. This meant that at one session everyone had to figure out a savings program that was appropriate for her own means and needs. At another session, each student was asked to look at her family's insurance coverage, and decide if more, less or a different kind of coverage was needed. In other words, my students learned by the most effective teaching technique there is: *by doing.*

This workbook is based on the same principle, and a glance at the table of contents will give you an idea of how it is organized. You'll begin with an introduction to financial planning, to learn what financial planning means, how to organize your current situation and how to set goals for the future. The next thirteen sections take you through specific areas of concern to most people—saving, borrowing, insurance, investing, retirement planning, estate planning and tax planning—but always within the context of *your* particular needs and objectives. When you get to the final section, Financial Planning in Action, you should be prepared to choose financial instruments and professional advisers that will help you achieve your objectives.

The workbook is not intended to be a definitive text on everything everyone will ever need to know about managing money. Rather,

I hope it gives women who were never before "interested in money" a start toward taking control of a new area in their lives and feeling pleased with themselves in the process.

—Carole Phillips
Wynnewood, Pennsylvania
January, 1982

The Money Workbook for Women

How Much Am I Worth: An Introduction to Financial Planning

Financial planning means making a comprehensive evaluation of your current financial situation, setting realistic goals for the future, and determining how to reach those goals.

Financial planning is the most effective way to organize our financial lives. It provides a structure within which we can think ahead, set goals, and coordinate the financial decisions that allow us to reach those goals.

The Financial Planning Process Takes Place in Five Steps

Step one—Getting organized

Step two—Setting goals

Step three—Developing a financial plan

Step four—Implementing the plan

Step five—Periodically reviewing and revising

Why Plan?
For peace of mind and financial security.

Joan, a 32-year-old unemployed office supervisor:

When I was working, I spent every penny I earned and more. I spent it on clothes, my apartment, vacations, you name it. If it had a price tag, I bought it. I had a good job with the government, but because of budget cutbacks, my department was closed. So there I was with a couple of hundred dollars in the bank, and a lot of bills to pay. I owe $2,000 on my car, and about $3,000 between the credit card and other bills. At first, it didn't bother me. I assumed I'd get another job. But it's been two months since I've worked, and now I'm scared. I can't sleep nights. When I go out for a job interview, I'm so tense and desperate, I know I make a terrible impression. And all I think about is how I wish I'd put away some money while I was making it.

Ruth, a 56-year-old widow:

When my husband was alive, he took care of me. I thought he would always take care of me. When he died, I discovered there was nothing left. He had borrowed on his insurance policy, and what Social Security gives you is not exactly what you would call extravagant. I still don't know where the money went. All I know is that I had to give up my house. I had to go out to work. I wasn't trained to do anything, and it's no picnic standing on my feet in a store all day.

Sheila, a 43-year-old homemaker:

I worry about our future. My husband, Paul, is a lawyer, and I know he makes a good living, but I don't know if we're doing the right thing with our investments. It's difficult to get him to sit down and talk about it. Sometimes we do nothing at all. The money just sits in the bank. Then Paul decides we've got to invest it, so he calls his stockbroker and we buy some stock. Sometimes we've done well, other times we've gotten badly burned. It's hard to know what to do. You get so much conflicting advice. One person says you should have a lot of insurance, another person says he doesn't believe in insurance. How do you know what to do? How do you know who to ask?"

Step One—Getting Organized

If Joan, Ruth or Sheila came to my office for counseling, the first thing I would ask her to do is fill in the Personal Financial Inventory on page 22 and the Personal Income Statement on page 28. This is step one of the financial planning process—getting organized. Then we move on to step two—setting goals. *We should not buy one single share of stock, one single insurance policy or any other financial asset until we know where we are and where we want to go.*

On first glance, the Inventory and Income Statement might appear overly time-consuming and complex. I promise you they're worth the investment of your time. It's instructive to see a picture of your total financial situation written down in one place, and you will have up-to-date information if you are asked to fill out an application for a loan or credit card. Also if you are married, or someone else manages money for you, researching the Inventory and Income Statement gives you a reason to ask questions you might have been reluctant to raise in the past. This is the first step toward peace of mind and financial security.

A Guide to the Personal Financial Inventory (see page 22)

The Personal Financial Inventory is like the balance sheet a business prepares to get a picture of its financial situation for a current time period.

Assets are listed on one side of the inventory, and *liabilities* on the other. Assets are everything you own, and liabilities are your debts or obligations to others. The difference between what you own and what you owe is your *net worth,* or what you are worth on the day you fill in the inventory.

Don't be concerned if some of the assets and liabilities listed are unfamiliar to you. They will be explained later in the workbook. Also, if you aren't certain what category an asset or liability fits in, write it down as "other." The important thing is to write everything down.

NOTE: Married women: Make three separate lists of assets and liabilities—those in your name alone, those in your husband's name, and those you own or owe together.

Assets

An asset is any financial or material possession that has monetary value. A savings account is an asset. So is the furniture in your home.

Liquid Assets (# 1)
Cash or assets which can be converted to cash quickly and easily with little uncertainty, such as Treasury bills and savings certificates. A

liquid asset has the same, or close to the same, value it had when you acquired it, plus interest earned in the interim.

Liquid assets are *marketable*. They can be sold outright (e.g., Treasury bills), or funds can be withdrawn as needed, such as from a savings account or money market fund.

NOTE: Some life insurance policies have a cash value for which the policy can be redeemed. The current cash value depends on the age of the policy, and is listed on a chart in the policy contract.

Other Marketable Assets (# 2)

Items such as real estate, stocks and bonds. These assets also can be sold, but at a price which might be more or less than you paid for them. Assets in this category usually are longer-term investments than liquid assets.

NOTE: List as "real estate" only property purchased as an investment. Your home, if you own one, should be included in the "nonmarketable assets" section. If you own stocks or bonds, ask a broker for their current value, or look up the prices in the newspaper (see page sixty-three).

Nonmarketable Assets (# 3)

Assets that have monetary value to the owner, but either cannot be sold, like your interest in a company pension fund, or else can be sold only through private negotiation, such as the sale of a dental practice or business.

NOTE: "Primary residence" and "vacation home" are included among nonmarketable assets because the houses we live in are not bought *primarily* as an investment.

Personal Property (# 4)

Assets purchased for personal use such as cars, books and jewelry. They should be included because this inventory is intended to convey your total "wealth."

After you've gone through each category—liquid assets, other marketable assets, nonmarketable assets, personal property—add the subtotals for the value of your TOTAL ASSETS (Line 5).

Liabilities

A liability is any financial obligation, or debt, to other individuals or institutional lenders. A loan from a relative or a loan from a bank is a liability. So is your home mortgage.

NOTE: List the *total amount* you owe currently under "credit card bills," "other household and personal bills," "loans" and "mortgages," even if you repay on an installment basis. The purpose of the Personal Financial Inventory is to give you an accurate picture of your current financial situation. If you paid off all your debts tomorrow, what would you be left with?

"Taxes due" are currently unpaid tax bills, such as a local real estate tax or sewer rent bill. Do not include income taxes unless they are past due.

Add up your liabilities for the value of your "total liabilities" (#6).

Net Worth

Deduct "total liabilities" from "total assets" to get your "net worth" (# 7), a picture in numbers of what you are worth today.

Personal Financial Inventory

_____
(date)

ASSETS	SELF	SPOUSE	JOINT	TOTAL
		OWNED BY		
1. Liquid assets	$ _____	$ _____	$ _____	$ _____
Checking accounts				
Savings accounts				
Credit union share accounts				
Savings Certificates				
U.S. savings bonds				
U.S. treasury bills				
Money market funds				
Life insurance cash value				
Other _____				
Total liquid assets	$ _____	$ _____	$ _____	$ _____
2. Other marketable assets				
Common stock				
Preferred stock				
Mutual funds				
U.S. notes & bonds				
Corporate notes & bonds				
Municipal bonds				
Real estate				
Gold & silver coins				
Collections (art, etc.)				
Other _____				
Total other marketable assets	$ _____	$ _____	$ _____	$ _____
3. Nonmarketable assets				
Vested interest pension plan				
Profit-sharing plan				
Individual retirement account				
Keogh plan				
Stock options				
Business interest				
Nonmarketable securities				

	SELF	SPOUSE	JOINT	TOTAL
Tax shelters	___	___	___	___
Annuities	___	___	___	___
Primary residence	___	___	___	___
Vacation home	___	___	___	___
Accounts receivable	___	___	___	___
Notes receivable	___	___	___	___
Other _____	___	___	___	___
Total nonmarketable assets	$___	$___	$___	$___

4. Personal property

	SELF	SPOUSE	JOINT	TOTAL
Automobiles	___	___	___	___
Household goods (furniture, etc.)	___	___	___	___
Jewelry & furs	___	___	___	___
Other _____	___	___	___	___
Total personal property	$___	$___	$___	$___
5. TOTAL ASSETS	$___	$___	$___	$___

LIABILITIES	OWED BY			
	SELF	SPOUSE	JOINT	TOTAL
Credit card bills	$___	$___	$___	$___
Other household & personal bills	___	___	___	___
Taxes due	___	___	___	___
Loans	___	___	___	___
1. _____	___	___	___	___
2. _____	___	___	___	___
3. _____	___	___	___	___
4. _____	___	___	___	___
Mortgages	___	___	___	___
1. _____	___	___	___	___
2. _____	___	___	___	___
Insurance policy loans	___	___	___	___
1. _____	___	___	___	___
2. _____	___	___	___	___
Other _____	___	___	___	___
6. TOTAL LIABILITIES	$___	$___	$___	$___

7. NET WORTH = Total assets−Total Liabilities

$$\$\_\_\_ \ = \ \$\_\_\_ \ - \ \$\_\_\_$$

The Personal Income Statement helps you see where your money comes from, where it goes, and how much you have left over to save or invest.

Prepare the income statement for the last full calendar year for which you have records.* Last year's tax return, your checkbook stubs and bank statements should have most of the information you need.

If you're married and have income of your own, list income and expenditures separately for yourself and your husband. If you don't have your own income, use the vertical "total" column for all calculations.

Income

List all sources of income, even those on which you pay no taxes, such as alimony or Social Security. "Non-taxable" interest is earned on securities such as municipal bonds, exempt from federal and some state income taxes. "Taxable" interest is earned on such savings instruments and investments as savings certificates, U.S. Treasury securities and corporate bonds.

Expenditures

Using the worksheet (see page 26), list expenditures for each month of the year. Transfer totals for each expenditure in the last right-hand column of the worksheet to the appropriate space on the income statement. (If you share expenses with a spouse or housemate, prepare two worksheets.)

Total income less total expenditures is, or should be, your *surplus for saving or investing.* If the difference is negative, it means you spent more than you earned.

NOTE: Examine your income and expenditure items. What can you do to increase your income or cut back on expenses *this* year?

Getting organized is step one of the financial planning process because we must know where we are today before we can say where we want to go tomorrow.

---

* If you expect your financial situation this year to differ significantly from last year, estimate the items that will be affected.

Where do *you* want to go?

Let's move on to step two—setting goals.

Step Two—Setting Goals

Before you begin to save and invest, you should know *why* you want financial assets and *how* you intend to use them.

Do you want to supplement your current income? Be financially independent? Are you concerned about retirement? Taxes? Inflation? Do you want to plan for your children's education or start your own business? Do you have a handicapped child or dependent parent whose security must be provided for?

Think about it. Write it down so you can *see* what you say you want. You can write down anything, so long as it's realistic for your financial situation. And list your goals in order of their importance to you. If you can't have or do everything you want, you can try to provide for the things you want most.

NOTE: Married women: Ask your husband to prepare a list of his financial goals. You will learn a great deal about one another's priorities when you compare his list with yours.

My Financial Goals

1. _____
2. _____
3. _____
4. _____
5. _____
6. _____
7. _____
8. _____
9. _____
10. _____
11. _____
12. _____
13. _____

	JAN	FEB	MAR	APR	MAY
Mortgage or rent	$ _____	$ _____	$ _____	$ _____	$ _____
Utilities					
Telephone					
Food					
Other household expenses					
Clothing					
Public transportation					
Car maintenance					
Gasoline for car(s)					
Medical & dental care					
Medicine & drugs					
Household cleaning					
Home maintenance					
Home decorating					
Life insurance premiums					
Disability insurance premiums					
Homeowner's insurance premiums					
Automobile insurance premiums					
Tuition					
Loan repayment—principal					
Loan repayment—interest					
Home entertainment					
Other entertainment					
Travel					
Charitable contributions					
Membership dues					
Newspapers					
Books					
Hobbies					
Federal income tax					
State income tax					
Local property tax					
Other taxes _____					
Other _____					
_____					
_____					
TOTAL	$ _____	$ _____	$ _____	$ _____	$ _____

penditures

JUNE	JULY	AUG	SEPT	OCT	NOV	DEC	TOTAL
$	$	$	$	$	$	$	$
$	$	$	$	$	$	$	$

Personal Income Statement—19___

Income	SELF	SPOUSE	JOINT	TOTAL
Wages and salaries	$ _____	$ _____	$ _____	$ _____
Tips	_____	_____	_____	_____
Commissions	_____	_____	_____	_____
Bonus/profit-sharing	_____	_____	_____	_____
Dividends	_____	_____	_____	_____
Taxable interest	_____	_____	_____	_____
Nontaxable interest	_____	_____	_____	_____
Rental income	_____	_____	_____	_____
Alimony	_____	_____	_____	_____
Child support	_____	_____	_____	_____
Social Security	_____	_____	_____	_____
Pension	_____	_____	_____	_____
Other _____	_____	_____	_____	_____
TOTAL INCOME	$ _____	$ _____	$ _____	$ _____

Expenditures	SELF	SPOUSE	JOINT	TOTAL
	$ _____	$ _____	$ _____	$ _____
Mortgage or rent	_____	_____	_____	_____
Utilities	_____	_____	_____	_____
Telephone	_____	_____	_____	_____
Food	_____	_____	_____	_____
Other household expenses	_____	_____	_____	_____
Clothing	_____	_____	_____	_____
Public transportation	_____	_____	_____	_____
Car maintenance	_____	_____	_____	_____
Gasoline for car(s)	_____	_____	_____	_____
Medical & dental care	_____	_____	_____	_____
Medicine & drugs	_____	_____	_____	_____
Household cleaning	_____	_____	_____	_____
Home maintenance	_____	_____	_____	_____
Home decorating	_____	_____	_____	_____
Life insurance premiums	_____	_____	_____	_____
Disability insurance premiums	_____	_____	_____	_____

Income	SELF	SPOUSE	JOINT	TOTAL
Homeowners insurance premiums	$ _____	$ _____	$ _____	$ _____
Automobile insurance premiums	_____	_____	_____	_____
Tuition(s)	_____	_____	_____	_____
Loan repayment—principal	_____	_____	_____	_____
Loan repayment—interest	_____	_____	_____	_____
Home entertainment	_____	_____	_____	_____
Other entertainment	_____	_____	_____	_____
Travel	_____	_____	_____	_____
Charitable contributions	_____	_____	_____	_____
Membership dues	_____	_____	_____	_____
Newspapers	_____	_____	_____	_____
Books	_____	_____	_____	_____
Hobbies	_____	_____	_____	_____
Federal income tax	_____	_____	_____	_____
State income tax	_____	_____	_____	_____
Local property tax	_____	_____	_____	_____
Other taxes _____	_____	_____	_____	_____
Other _____	_____	_____	_____	_____
_____	_____	_____	_____	_____
_____	_____	_____	_____	_____
_____	_____	_____	_____	_____
_____	_____	_____	_____	_____
_____	_____	_____	_____	_____
_____	_____	_____	_____	_____
_____	_____	_____	_____	_____

TOTAL EXPENDITURES $ _____ $ _____ $ _____ $ _____

SURPLUS FOR SAVING & INVESTING
(TOTAL INCOME – TOTAL EXPENDITURES)

$ _____ $ _____ $ _____ $ _____

How and Where to Hold Your Nest Egg

Everyone should set aside a nest egg of savings that can be counted on for emergencies.

Think of this savings nest egg as "self-insurance," your most certain and immediate source of financial security. It's your buffer to live on between jobs, the way to pay an old-fashioned plumber who insists on cash when the pipes burst, the money you always know will be there if you need it.

The money in your nest egg must be *safe* and *liquid*. Safety means there is little or no risk of loss. Liquidity means having access to cash as soon as you need it. You want to earn the highest *interest* (return or yield) you can on savings, but yield is secondary to safety and liquidity.

Safe and liquid interest-earning savings instruments are listed on pages 34–37. (They also are listed among "liquid assets" on the Personal Financial Inventory on page 22.) You might use these same savings instruments to provide for other financial goals, but the higher-risk non-liquid investments you will consider for other financial goals are not suitable for a savings nest egg.

How Much Should You Keep in Your Savings Nest Egg?

One rule-of-thumb is that you should accumulate over several years the equivalent of one-quarter of your after-tax income.*

---

* After-tax income also is referred to as net income, disposable income or take-home pay.

Whether you save more or less depends on other assets you own, job security and family responsibilities.

This is a *target* figure, not an amount you must save each year. If you must draw upon your savings nest egg in an emergency, build it up again as soon as possible.

Calculate Your Savings Goal

		EXAMPLE
My (our) after-tax income for 19__	$_____	$20,000
	× ¼ =	× ¼ =
My (our) accumulated savings should be	$_____	$ 5,000

The Married Woman's Nest Egg

Sandy and Laura keep joint savings accounts with their husbands for family emergencies. They also have savings accounts of their own that is *their* money to do with as they please.

Sandy, a high school English teacher, has a deposit made from her paycheck to her share account in the teacher's credit union every payday. Laura, a homemaker, makes a deposit out of her household money at the savings bank next to the supermarket before she does her weekly food shopping every Friday.

If Sandy and Laura save $10 a week for 50 weeks, at the end of a year they will have $520 including interest. If they can save $20 each week, they'll have $1,040 including interest. It is a good beginning. If Laura does nothing more than keep the money in a savings account earning 5½%, $1,000 will be worth more than $1,300 in five years. And if she puts $1,000 into her account every year for five years, at the end of five years she will have almost $6,000. By that time, her two children will be in school full-time, and perhaps she will use her savings to go back to college or start her own business.

Whether you work outside or in the home, it's easy to get started on a savings program of your own. Just take "The Saver's Pledge."

The Saver's Pledge

_____
(date)

I promise to save $____ per week each week until _____,
19—, at which time I shall have $_____.

Signed,

_____
(your name)

Where Should You Keep Your Nest Egg?

The savings instruments you should consider are listed below. The savings instruments you should _choose_ are the ones that are right for your preferences and needs.

Carol and Mike have four children, and barely make it from paycheck to paycheck. They received a $5,000 inheritance. They used $2,000 to pay some bills, and bought a $3,000 savings certificate. They know their money will be "frozen" in the certificate for two and a half years, and that interest rates might move higher than the rate at which they are "locked in," but they prefer the security of an insured certificate to the more liquid, potentially higher-yielding money market fund.

Lucy and Alec, on the other hand, have a joint income of $75,000 and a combined net worth of over $200,000. Each has a money market fund account and an All-Savers tax-exempt savings certificate. They want maximum liquidity and high pre-tax yield for part of their savings, safety and maximum after-tax yield for the other part.

And then there is Alice, who retired recently from her well-paying job as senior buyer for a major Chicago department store. She closed her tax-free money market fund account and bought a six-month Treasury bill because she now is in a lower tax bracket and will keep more of the higher pre-tax yield.

Everyone's needs are different.

Savings Instruments and Where to Buy Them

NOTE: Terms and rates on current saving instruments change frequently, and new savings vehicles are being introduced all the time. Check things out with your depositing institution or stock broker before you buy.

Passbook Savings Account

A savings account for which deposits, withdrawals and interest are recorded by the depository institution each time a transaction is made. A passbook account is liquid and safe but has a relatively low yield.

Available at commercial banks, savings banks, savings & loan associations (S&L's) *

Statement Savings Account

A savings account for which the account holder keeps her own records of deposits, withdrawals and interest. Receipts and quarterly statements are provided by the depository institution as confirmations of transactions; a statement savings account might pay a higher interest rate than a passbook account. It is liquid and safe but has a relatively low yield.

Available at commercial banks, savings banks, S&L's.

Credit Union Share Account

Savings account in a credit union, available only to credit union members. Credit unions are permitted to pay higher rates than banks and S&L's, but funds must be kept in an account for one month or more to earn interest. Share accounts are liquid and safe, with a relatively low-to-medium yield range.

Available at credit unions.

Savings Certificate

A contractual agreement that a saver will keep a specific amount of money in a depository institution for one to ten years and receive a specific rate of interest. Certificates pay higher rates of interest than regular savings accounts. Some interest, and perhaps a part of the principal, is lost if a certificate is redeemed before its maturity date. Savings certificates are safe, relatively liquid with a medium-to-high yield range.

Available at commercial banks, savings institutions, credit unions.

"Money Market" Certificate

A savings certificate issued for six months for a minimum of $10,000. The interest rate is ¼ % more than the current six-month U.S.

---

* Savings banks and S&L's are sometimes referred to collectively as savings or thrift institutions.

Treasury bill rate. Ninety days interest is lost if a money market certificate is redeemed before its maturity date. A money market certificate is safe, relatively liquid and relatively high yielding.

Available at commercial banks, savings institutions, credit unions.

Tax-Exempt (All-Savers) Savings Certificate

A one-year savings certificate issued for a minimum of $500. The interest rate is 70 % of the current one-year U.S. Treasury bill rate. A maximum of $1,000 a year ($2,000 on joint returns) is exempt from federal income tax. No more than $1,000 interest ($2,000 on joint returns) may be exempted during one's lifetime on this kind of certificate. The tax exemption is lost and there is an interest penalty on early redemptions. Tax-exempt savings certificate will be sold until December 31, 1982. Tax-exempt certificates are safe, relatively liquid with the after-tax-equivalent yield dependent on the buyer's tax bracket. Insured by the FDIC, FSLIC or NCUA for up to $100,000.

Available at commercial banks, savings institutions, credit unions.

U.S. Treasury Bill

Issued by the U.S. Treasury for 3, 6, 9 and 12 month periods for a minimum of $10,000 with $5,000 increments. Treasury bills are safe, relatively liquid, and relatively high yielding.

"T-bills" can be purchased from a regional Federal Reserve Bank (no service charge) or a commercial bank or stockbroker (service charge).

Money Market Fund

A mutual fund which purchases large-denomination money market instruments, such as Treasury bills and bank-issued certificates of deposit. The interest earned, which can be higher than the rates paid on savings accounts, is passed along to the shareholders. Money market fund interest rates change as the yields on the securities in their portfolio change. The minimum investment is as low as $300 to $1,000. There is no sales charge for purchase or redemption of fund shares. Share prices remain the same at all times. There is no minimum holding period. Money market funds are safe, but not as safe as insured savings instruments. They are liquid and relatively high yielding.

Purchased directly from a fund or through a stockbroker.

Tax-Free Money Market Fund

A money market fund which makes investments that earn interest exempt from federal, and some state, income taxes. The minimum investment is $1,000 to $20,000. Tax-free money market funds are safe, but not as safe as insured instruments. They are liquid, and the after-tax-equivalent yield depends on the shareholder's tax bracket.

Purchased directly from a fund or through a stockbroker.

Savings Bonds

Savings bonds are the smallest denominated government bonds.

Series EE savings bonds are sold for a minimum of $25 with a $50 redemption value at nine-year maturity. Series HH savings bonds are sold for a minimum of $500 with interest paid semiannually and a ten-year maturity.

Both Series EE and Series HH bonds may be cashed in six months after issue date. The stated interest rate is paid only on bonds held to maturity. A lower yield in the form of a lower redemption value is paid on bonds cashed in prior to the maturity date. No interest is paid on Series EE bonds held less than a year or Series HH bonds held less than six months.

Investors with $500 or more should buy higher yielding savings instruments and bonds rather than savings bonds. Investors with less than $500 should keep their money in a savings account or share account until they have accumulated the funds needed to buy a higher yielding savings instrument or bond.

Where to Keep Transaction Balances*

Transaction balances are what we use to call checking account balances, that is, the money you use to pay bills or other financial obligations. Now that you can earn interest directly on transaction balances, or transfer money instantly from an interest-paying savings account to a noninterest-earning checking account, *all* your money can be working for you *all the time*. Transaction accounts are offered by the same depository institutions that provide savings instruments.

NOW Account

Acronym for Negotiable Order of Withdrawal, or a checking account that earns interest. Depository institutions either require a mini-

---

* One of the ways a married woman can establish an independent financial identity is by opening her own transaction account.

mum balance, charge for each transaction, charge a monthly maintenance fee, or some combination of the three.

Credit Union Share Drafts
Checks that credit union members may write against their interest-earning share accounts.

Telephone Transfer
A depository institution that holds your savings account transfers
funds to your checking account, either in the same or in another depository institution, when you request the transfer by telephone. There is a
follow-up confirmation by mail. Usually a minimum amount is required for transfers. There might be a small transfer charge.

Telephone Bill-Paying Account
A depository institution is provided with a list of creditors you
pay frequently, e.g., mortgage or rent, utility bills, insurance premiums, department stores, etc. You continue to receive bills from the
creditors. You telephone the depository institution and authorize payments from your savings account of specific amounts to each creditor's
checking or savings account in the same or in another institution. The
depository institution provides a confirmation of each transaction.
There is a small charge for each transaction.

A Savings Account Accessed by Automatic Teller Machine (ATM)
Through the use of a plastic card and a secret number, you may
transfer funds from an interest-earning savings account to a noninterest-earning checking account in the same or different depository institution. ATM's usually are open 24 hours a day, 7 days a week, and
are found in many convenient locations.

Direct Deposit
Payroll, Social Security, and other government checks can be
deposited directly into your interest-earning transaction or savings
account.

Money Market Fund
Checks, usually with an allowable minimum of $500, may be
written against your fund account. You earn interest until the check
clears the fund's bank. A few funds permit access to your fund account
with credit cards.

Whether a Borrower You Should Be

Three questions to ask before *you* go into debt:

Do I (we) really need to borrow?   Yes ☐   No ☐

Can I (we) afford to repay what I (we) borrow?   Yes ☐   No ☐

Can I (we) bear the emotional burden of being in
debt?   Yes ☐   No ☐

NOTE: We include *borrowing* in the financial planning process because the amount you borrow and the terms on which you borrow (interest rate, repayment schedule, maturity of loan) affect the attainment of the long-term goals you set on pages 31 through 33.

One of Laura's goals was to return to college. She did not want to wait until she had saved all the money she needed for tuition. She borrowed $1,000 from her savings bank, using her savings account as security for the loan. She thinks this is a good investment in her future.

Peter and Susan have joint incomes of $30,000 a year. They want to buy a house, but they cannot get a mortgage. Because they have borrowed so heavily on their bank credit card and are paying off two late-model cars, the mortgage lender says they do not have adequate income to cover mortgage payments and other housing expenses.

How Much Can You Afford to Borrow?

Divide: $\dfrac{\$ \text{\_\_\_\_\_ (monthly debt repayment)}}{\$ \text{\_\_\_\_\_ (one month's income before taxes)}}$ = _____ % of monthly income owed to creditors

Is this more, less or about the right amount of debt you can afford to repay now and in the future? If you lost your job or other sources of income, could you raise the cash to pay off your debts? The liquid assets and other marketable assets listed in the Personal Financial Inventory on page 22 are your sources of cash.

If You Plan to Borrow, but Before You Sign up for One of the Loans or Credit Arrangements Discussed on the Next Page

• Complete the Personal Income Statement (page thirteen) and Personal Financial Inventory (page eight). You will be asked for some or all of this information by a lender or credit card issuer.

• Keep in mind that if a woman meets credit requirements on her own, lenders and credit card issuers are not permitted to require husbands or fathers to co-sign for loans.

• Understand that lenders and credit card issuers must take all sources of income into account—alimony, child support, Social Security, part-time work, investment income, etc.—in evaluating an applicant's creditworthiness.

• Get acquainted with a bank officer where you have your checking or savings account. If someone knows you and is willing to vouch for your good character, it can make the difference between acceptance and rejection when work history and income level are on the borderline for the lender's credit guidelines.

• Comparison shop. Rates and terms vary among lenders.

• Know the *real* percentage rate at which you borrow; it may be different from the stated rate. For example:

Your loan may be *discounted.* This means if you borrow $1,000 at 12% for one year, $120 (12% of $1,000) is deducted immediately. You get the use of only $880, but repay $1,000. The *ef-*

fective or *real* rate is then 13.63% ($120 divided by $880 = 13.63%).

Where to Borrow*

If you are going to finance such major expenditures as a car or home repairs, you might apply for a *consumer loan* at a commercial bank, savings institution, credit union or consumer finance company. Generally, consumer loan rates are lowest at credit unions and highest at finance companies.

A consumer loan can be an *installment loan,* which means a part of the loan plus interest are re-paid monthly. Or, only interest can be paid monthly, with total principal repaid at maturity. Consumer loans often are secured (require collateral). If the borrower defaults, the lender has the right to take possession of the collateral (e.g., the car being paid off; stocks or bonds).

The least expensive kind of consumer loan is the *passbook loan* made by savings banks and S&L's. The loan is secured by funds in a passbook (or statement) savings account. From 90 to 100% of the savings account balance may be borrowed, usually at a rate only 1 to 2% higher than the savings rate. Borrowers continue to earn interest on their savings, although an amount in the account equal to the amount of the outstanding loan is "frozen" until the loan is repaid. This means the real cost of borrowing is the difference between the interest you earn and the interest you pay. Most people who *borrow* rather than *use* their own savings do so because they find it easier to repay a loan than to rebuild their savings nest egg.

Another inexpensive source of borrowed funds has been *life insurance policies.* The owner of a whole life insurance policy may borrow the cash value of the policy. This amount, always less than the amount of insurance that would be paid on the death of the insured, is found in a table in the policy contract. There is no requirement to repay the loan, only the interest. If the loan remains unpaid and the insured dies, the amount of the loan is deducted from the proceeds the beneficiary receives. Interest rates on life insurance loans range be-

* Because they are a specialized and long-term kind of borrowing, home mortgages are discussed in Section 6.

tween 5% and 8%. You must contact an insurance agent or the insurance company to apply for a policy loan.

One of the oldest kinds of consumer credit is *revolving credit*. A customer arranges with a retail store or other vendor to pay off a coat, a refrigerator, or whatever, at a specific rate of interest during a specific period of time. Interest rates on revolving credit purchases are comparable to rates charged on credit card purchases. A maximum allowable interest rate on consumer credit often is set by state law, and varies from state to state.

Credit card purchases and *cash advances* are among the most expensive kinds of consumer credit. Their appeal is that they permit relatively small or odd sums of money to be borrowed at the borrower's discretion. No application or waiting period is required after the account is opened.

Credit cards issued by merchants, oil companies, banks and other financial service organizations may be used to purchase goods and services. Credit card purchases may be paid for when the monthly bill is presented for payment, or paid off in monthly installments plus an interest charge. A cardholder's outstanding purchases may be limited by the dollar amount of a maximum credit line. An annual "membership fee" or monthly service fee may be charged.

Some card issuers permit cardholders to receive cash advances. The cash is obtained from an office of the card issuer, another financial organization or a variety of electronic dispensers. The amount of a cash advance may be limited to the amount of the cardholder's credit line less the amount of outstanding purchases. In some states, the interest rate charged on a cash advance is less than the interest rate charged on purchases.

Some banks and savings institutions permit certain customers to "overdraw" their checking accounts up to a preauthorized dollar limit. Interest is charged only on borrowed funds. The credit line might be made available only to bank credit card customers or to all creditworthy checking account cutomers. The interest rate charged usually is less or the same as the rate on credit card cash advances.

Application Rejected

Not every application for a loan or credit card is accepted. Prospective borrowers or cardholders must prove they are able and willing to pay their debts.

The federal Equal Credit Opportunity Act says that all credit applications must be judged by the same criteria and prohibits discrimination against prospective borrowers because of their age, race or sex.

Yet there still are occasions when a young woman is told she must have her father co-sign her loan note, or a widow over 65-years-old is refused credit because her age makes her ineligible for credit insurance.

What can women do in such cases?

If You Think Your Application for a Credit Card Was Rejected Because You Are Female, if You Think Your Male Counterpart (Same Age, Income, Marital Status, Employment Record) Would Have Received Credit and You Didn't

• Ask why you were rejected. If you are told the rejection was based on information received from a credit bureau, request a copy of your credit record (see page 44).

• Know your rights under the Equal Credit Opportunity Act. Consult a copy of the act. Every financial institution is required to keep copies for customers' use.

• Ask the loan officer or credit card company employee to reconsider his (her) decision. Tell him (her) you are familiar with the Act, and that you believe you were rejected without cause.

If You Receive No Satisfaction

Write a letter specifying your complaint, or have your attorney write, to the president of the organization that rejected your application. Send a copy of your letter to your state or local department of consumer affairs. Make certain that the president of the lending institution knows you are sending this copy.

If You Receive No Satisfaction
Ask the state or local department of consumer affairs for help.

If You Receive No Satisfaction
Ask for the name of the state or federal agency with regulatory responsibilities for the organization that rejected your application. File a complaint with that agency.

How to Check Your Credit Record

If you have credit cards or outstanding loans, there probably is a file on you at a local credit bureau. The information in your file is supplied by organizations that have extended credit to you, such as banks and retail stores. If you are curious about the information the bureau is disclosing about you, you may request a copy of your file.

• Ask your bank for the name of the local credit bureau it uses.

• Call the credit bureau and request a file disclosure form. There is no fee for the form if you have been denied credit within the past 30 days; otherwise, a small fee is charged.

• Return the file disclosure form.

• You will receive a credit report with the following information (usually in barely decipherable computerese):

A list of past and current debts to retail stores, credit card issuers and other creditors.

How quickly you pay your bills.

Whether and why you have been refused credit.

Whether you have declared bankruptcy.

Whether you are delinquent or have defaulted on a student loan.

Any experiences with creditors' attorneys or collection agencies.

Other information filed by and of interest to creditors.

- Inform the credit bureau in writing if there is inaccurate information on your credit report. The bureau is supposed to confirm your contention and make the necessary changes on your record. Apply for another credit report to make certain it's been done.

Why a Married Woman Should Have a Credit Record in Her Own Name

No one should borrow or get a credit card simply for the sake of establishing a credit record. But if you have legitimate needs for a loan or credit card, there are several reasons why married women, even those who have no income of their own, should establish independent financial identities.

The Grim Statistics

- There were 22 million widows and divorcees in the U.S. in 1980.

- Only 40% of women widowed in their 30s, 19% of women widowed in their 40s, 9% of women widowed in their 50s, and 5% of widows 60 years old or older remarry.

- 85% of married women will be widowed or divorced.

If you are widowed or divorced and have financial accounts in your own name, you are spared the burden of closing old accounts and opening new ones under emotionally trying circumstances. But if you have no previous credit record or if your financial situation has changed, your credit application for a new account might be rejected.

The Best Way to Learn Is by Doing

If it's *your* bank account or credit card, it's *your* responsibility.

If it's your responsibility, you are more likely to monitor and actively manage financial matters than to "let George do it."

The Satisfaction of Having Control over Your Financial Well-Being

Nobody, not even a kind and generous husband, looks out for your interests as well as you do yourself. In fact, many men have neither the time nor the interest for active money management and keeping up with new financial services. Women who are experienced family budgeters quickly learn to deal with financial institutions the same way they deal with vendors of other goods and services: searching out and getting the best possible service at the best possible price.

To Establish
Your Credit Rating

• Open your own checking and savings account or an interest-paying transaction account.

• Make a passbook loan from your savings account (see page 41).

• Have credit cards imprinted with your name (Barbara Harrison, *not* Mrs. Frank Harrison).

• Request that credit records for joint accounts be kept separately for both spouses. As an individual account-holder, even a woman who has no income of her own may establish a track record as a reliable and responsible borrower. The *willingness* to repay closely follows the *ability* to repay as a requirement among lenders and card issuers for good credit risks.

• Request a preauthorized credit line on your checking account (see page 46).

Use the credit line to make a substantial purchase, such as a stereo or airplane tickets. The money to pay for the stereo or tickets might come from your husband, but *you* get the Brownie points for repaying the loan.

• If income-producing assets, such as stocks, bonds, or savings accounts, can be transferred from your husband or a joint account to your name alone, you might have adequate income to qualify for your own bank credit card, retail store account, or gasoline credit card. (Even if she's not applying for credit, every married woman should have assets in her own name (see page 42).

Nobody Knows What's Coming Tomorrow: Life and Disability Insurance*

Why buy life insurance?

The more dependent others are on you and the less other assets you have, the more life insurance you need. The less dependent others are on you and the more other assets you have, the less life insurance you need.

Whether you buy life insurance, and the amount you buy, depends on how you would want the proceeds of a policy to be used.

Alice is divorced and the mother of 12-year-old twins. While her ex-husband, who has remarried, contributes to the children's support, she is not certain he would be willing to pay for the whole of their college tuitions if she were not around to pay her share. Alice uses insurance to assure her children of the education she wants them to have.

Harriet is single and has no dependents now, but in the future inflation might make it necessary for Harriet to supplement her widowed mother's pension and Social Security. An insurance policy on Harriet's life will provide that additional income if her mother outlives Harriet.

Tom and Elaine were able to buy a condominium only because their combined incomes could be used to pay off the mortgage. If one of them died, the other would be forced to sell the apartment. They have insurance for the specific purpose of keeping a roof over the head of the surviving spouse.

* Property and liability insurance are not discussed in this workbook. However, if you own property which is insurable against loss, theft or damage, such as a car or house, or if you could be held responsible (i.e., liable) for other persons being injured or their property damaged, then you should investigate the appropriate insurance coverage.

Most life insurance proceeds are paid to beneficiaries when an insured person dies. Some policies combine savings with death benefits; that is, if the insured person lives to be a certain age a lump sum or periodic income payments are paid out.

Life insurance should not be purchased as an investment. In the long run, if you follow a regular savings and investment program, you probably will earn a better rate of return than you would using the same money to pay insurance premiums over the same period of time.

The advantage of life insurance over other investments is that insurance proceeds are paid if you die before you have had the time to accumulate the funds you want for specific goals that benefit other people. Life insurance guarantees protection for the people dependent on you for financial support.

How Much Life Insurance Do You Need?

There are two kinds of financial obligations to be met: (1) one-time or lump sum *capital* needs and (2) on-going *income* needs. Calculate your income and capital needs according to your current situation.

What Kind of Life Insurance Should You Buy?

The three main kinds of life insurance are *whole life, term,* and *endowment* policies. There is also a new type of insurance called *universal life.*

Whole Life

When you buy a whole life, permanent life, straight life or ordinary life insurance policy, you are insured from the day the policy begins to the day you die. Premiums* may be paid throughout your

---

* The *premium* is your payment to the insurance company for the insurance coverage it provides. Premiums may be paid monthly, quarterly, semiannually or annually.

lifetime, for a limited time period, such as 20 years (limited payment life), or, less commonly, in one payment.

A percentage of the premiums you pay, called the cash value, accumulates somewhat like a savings account. If you stopped paying premiums, you would receive the cash value at that time. You may *borrow* the cash value at any time, but the benefits of the policy (what would be paid to your beneficiaries) decreases by the amount borrowed.*

Individuals who no longer need or who cannot afford a high level of whole life coverage have three options if they wish to reduce or eliminate premiums:

1. Termination of the policy by withdrawing the cash value and investing the proceeds at higher rates of interest than the insurance company pays.

2. Extended term option. The policy shifts from a whole life contract to a term contract. The policy has the same face value, but the premiums are lower and the policy now runs for a specific period of time instead of the insured's lifetime.†

3. Paid-up whole life. The policy continues, but at a lower face value (lower benefits to beneficiaries).† There are no more premium payments.

Term Insurance

As the name implies, term insurance provides insurance coverage for a specific period of time; e.g., five or ten years. A new policy must be purchased when the old policy expires if you want to be insured.

The cost of a new term insurance policy increases as you get older, but term insurance offers lower cost coverage than whole life insurance at every age.

There is no cash value build-up with a term policy, only the face value which is paid to beneficiaries if the insured dies before the policy terminates.

Group insurance policies provided as employee benefits are term policies. Coverage ends when an employee leaves the company.

---

* Cash and loan values for each year you own a policy are printed in the tables of cash, loan and other values in all whole life contracts.

† Terms and face values for each year you own a policy are printed in the tables of cash, loan and other values in all whole life contracts.

How Much Life Insurance Do You Need?

1. One-time or lump sum capital needs after death:

Final expenses*:

Funeral expenses	$_____	$ 3,000
Medical expanses not covered by health insurance	$_____	$ 1,000
Estate and inheritance taxes	$_____	$ 0
Lawyer's & executor's fees	$_____	$ 1,000
TOTAL FINAL EXPENSES	$_____	$ 5,000

Children's college tuition:

$24,000 for 4 years for 2 children	$_____	$ 48,000
Pay off home mortgages	$_____	$ 30,000
Other capital needs	$_____	$ 0
TOTAL CAPITAL NEEDS	$_____	$ 83,000

Deduct funds available to meet capital needs:

Assets (page 19—exclude cash value of life insurance)	$_____	$ 25,000
Pension fund survivors' benefits	$_____	$ 10,000
Other _____	$_____	$ 0
Funds available to meet capital needs	$_____	$ 35,000

LIFE INSURANCE TO MEET CAPITAL NEEDS	$_____	$ 48,000

2. On-going income needs after death:

Annual income needs of spouse, children or other dependents	$_____ /year	$ 20,000 /year
Annual income needed to pay for housekeeping & child care services	$_____ /year	$ 5,000 /year
Other _____	$_____ /year	$ 0 /year
TOTAL ON-GOING INCOME NEEDS	$_____ /year	$ 25,000 /year

* Consult an insurance agent or estate planner for a realistic estimate applicable to your own situation.

Deduct annual income received from:

Social Security survivors' benefits	$_____ /year	$ 8,000 /year
Veterans' Survivors' benefits	$_____ /year	$ 2,000 /year
Pension fund survivors' benefits (if paid out in installments)	$_____ /year	$ 0 /year
Other _____	$_____ /year	$ 0 /year
TOTAL	$_____ /year	$ 10,000 /year

On-going income needs to be met with life
    insurance $_____ /year $ 15,000 /year

3. Calculate life insurance required to meet annual income needs:

Assume rate of interest that can be earned   ____ %   8%

Divide:

Income needs to be met with life insurance $____ (1) $ 15,000
    divide by

Assume rate of return and multiply by 1000 $____ % (2)   8%
    Equals

Life insurance to meet annual income needs $____ (3) $187,500

Check: ___% (2) × $_____ (3) = ____ (1)

                8% × $187,500 = $15,000

Combine:

Life insurance to meet capital needs $____ (1) $ 48,000
    and

Life insurance to meet annual income $____ (2) $187,500
needs

        ESTIMATED TOTAL LIFE
           INSURANCE NEEDED† $____ (3) $235,500

NOTE: Although principal might be used if necessary, it is safer to try to keep the principal intact and live off of the income it generates.

† If you buy this amount of life insurance, can you afford to pay the premiums? If not, cut back to the level at which essential and immediate needs would be met.

One drawback to a term policy is that the policy might terminate while the need to protect dependents remains. A term policy is not automatically renewed. And because it is necessary to prove "insurability" each time a term policy is purchased, an insured who becomes "uninsurable" might not qualify for continued coverage.

However, there are two clauses that can be inserted in a term policy at a small additional charge to protect against rejection because of "noninsurability":

1. A renewability clause which guarantees your right to renew a term policy a certain number of times; that is, you may have the option to renew a 5-year term policy five terms or 25 years.

2. A convertibility clause which permits conversion of a term policy to a whole life policy during the time period the term insurance is in effect.

Decreasing term insurance is a variety of term insurance often purchased as mortgage insurance on a home or tuition insurance for children's education. The face value of a decreasing term policy decline as the outstanding value of the mortgage or tuition obligations decrease. If the insured dies before the mortgage is repaid or the child's education completed, the policy proceeds are used to pay off the mortgage or pay the tuition.

A decreasing term policy intended as mortgage insurance should be written as a general policy so that a surviving spouse or other beneficiaries have the *option* to pay off the mortgage. If current interest rates are higher than the mortgage rate, the beneficiaries might want to invest the insurance proceeds and continue to make mortgage payments.

Endowment Policies

An endowment policy is intended to be a combination of term insurance and savings. The insurance is in effect for a specific number of years. If the insured dies while the policy is in effect, the face value of the policy is paid to its beneficiaries. If the insured outlives the insurance period, the face value plus accumulated interest is paid to the insured, in one lump sum payment or in periodic installments.

Although popular at one time, endowment policies now seem to offer less insurance coverage than term insurance for the price and the same number of years, and a lower rate of interest on the "savings" than an individual could earn by placing the funds spent on premiums in other investments.

Universal Life

The most attractive feature of this new kind of life insurance is the possibility of earning a higher rate of interest on the accumulated cash value than traditional whole life policies pay. A larger accumulation of cash leaves larger death benefits for beneficiaries than whole life policies even if the policy owner has borrowed or withdrawn part of the cash value. Also, some universal life policies pay the accumulated cash value in addition to the face value of a policy as a death benefit to beneficiaries.

As with term insurance, universal life coverage can be increased or reduced according to the insured's responsibilities and financial status at different times in his or her life. Unlike term insurance, which expires after a certain number of years, a universal policy remains in effect as long as the policy owner makes premium payments or there is sufficient cash value to cover annual premiums.

Naming the Players:
Owners and Beneficiaries
of Life Insurance Policies

The *owner* of a life insurance policy is the person who has the *rights of ownership:* to assign (transfer ownership of) the policy to another person; to name or change beneficiaries; to terminate the policy; to withdraw the cash value; to borrow the cash value; and to change the premium payment periods (whether premiums should be paid monthly, quarterly or yearly).

The owner of an insurance policy might be, but does not have to be, the person whose life is insured by the policy (the insured).

Also, the owners of the policy might be the same or different from the policy's *beneficiaries,* the persons who receive the proceeds of the policy upon the death of the insured. *Named beneficiaries are not required to pay income tax on life insurance proceeds.*

It is not *necessary* for a woman with no income of her own who owns a policy on her husband's life to write the checks to pay the premium, but many financial advisors suggest that she do so to establish evidence of ownership should the husband's estate be audited by the Internal Revenue Service.

NOTE: Before the passage of the 1981 Tax Act, many married

people assigned (transferred ownership of) their insurance policies to their spouses or an unfunded insurance trust (discussed in Section 11). Otherwise, if the insured retained ownership, the policy proceeds could be subject to estate taxes. Because the Tax Act permits an unlimited amount of assets to be passed tax-free to a spouse after January 1, 1982, a married woman might want to retain ownership of her insurance policy during her lifetime and bequeath the policy to her husband in her will.

Payment of Life Insurance Proceeds

Either the owner or the beneficiary of an insurance policy decides how the proceeds of a policy are to be paid to the beneficiary. The choices, called *settlement options,* are to receive a lump sum distribution or periodic payments.

The advantage of a lump sum distribution is that the beneficiary has immediate control and use of the funds. They may be spent on pressing personal needs, invested, or used to pay estate settlement expenses, such as taxes or lawyers' fees.

If periodic payments are made, the insurance company pays interest on the undistributed portion of the proceeds, but usually at a lower rate than the beneficiary could earn by investing conservatively in savings instruments (see Section 2) or bonds (see Section 5). Also, if a periodic payment option is chosen, and the beneficiary dies before the final distribution is made, some companies reduce the rate of interest paid to the beneficiary's beneficiaries.

If You Are Married and the Beneficiary of Your Husband's Insurance Policy, Remember

• Many widows who receive insurance payments are bombarded by fast-talking salespeople offering "golden investment opportunities" that must be taken advantage of immediately. Well-meaning friends and stockbrokers will call with advice about "what you should do with your money."

• Do nothing which you might later regret. No important financial decision should be made under such difficult emotional circumstances as the recent death of a husband. The best thing a widow can do with an insurance payment is put it in a safe, liquid savings instrument until she feels ready to think clearly and rationally about her long-term needs.

How to Apply for Payment of a Life Insurance Policy

• If you have the responsibility of collecting life insurance proceeds, contact the insurance agent who sold the policy. He or she should be able to guide you through the collection process.

• If you do not know the agent, write directly to the insurance company. The name and address is printed on the policy. Request an insurance claim application, providing the decedent's name, a copy of the death certificate, the insurance policy number, and your name and address.

• You will receive a form which must be signed by the policy's beneficiary and, if the owner has provided the option, which will ask the beneficiary to choose between a lump sum or periodic payment distribution.

• Keep copies of all correspondence with the insurance company.

• A check for the lump sum payment or the first installment payment should be sent two to four weeks after the claim is filed.

• If you have any problems or feel that the company is not handling your claim properly, contact the regulatory agency for insurance in your state.

Do Not Buy

Insurance at Airports
"If you need insurance at the airport, you need insurance, period."
—Ann Costello, Department of Finance and Insurance, University of Hartford.

Women who travel frequently should consider special insurance policies that provide coverage if death occurs while traveling.

Some credit card issuers provide life insurance at low or no charge if your air fare is charged to the credit card. Also, a special provision for insurance coverage while traveling on company business is included in some employers' group insurance plans.

NOBODY KNOWS WHAT'S COMING TOMORROW

Cancer Insurance

"When death occurs as a result of cancer, a family has tremendous medical expenses. But the fact is there are tremendous medical expenses if someone dies from kidney disease or heart disease. The situation is the same as with airport insurance. Why not have death protection for all diseases if the need for insurance is there?" (Ann Costello.)

Disability Insurance

When Patsy the Plumber or **Nancy** the Nurse becomes disabled, not only does her income go ↓ but expenses go ↑.

The chances of being incapacitated and unable to work are higher than the probability of death at every age level for preretirement age workers.*

Different Definitions of "Disabled" Used by Insurance Companies in Their Policies

1. Confined to bed; totally incapacitated.

2. Unable to work at *any* occupation.

3. Unable to work at a specific occupation.

NOTE: #3 is most desirable coverage.

When Should Disability Payments Begin and How Long Should They Last?†

The purpose of disability insurance is to replace lost earnings.

Generally, the sooner payments begin, the more expensive the policy. Also, the longer the period of coverage, the more expensive the policy.

---

* A woman must be employed outside the home to be covered by disability insurance. If you're a homemaker with two small children and break your leg, you won't qualify. But make certain your husband is insured, and watch where you walk.
† Before planning your disability income needs, check to see if disability insurance is provided to you as an employee benefit.

Recommended: A long-term disability policy that becomes effective six months to a year after a worker is incapacitated and continues until retirement benefits become effective.

Be sure to have savings and adequate health insurance to protect yourself and your family until disability payments begin.

How Much Disability Insurance Do You Need?

60 to 70% of your current annual income after taxes* $_____

DEDUCT: Income from savings & investments $_____
   Social Security disability benefits _____
   Workman's Compensation   _____
   Employer-provided disability benefits _____
           TOTAL $_____

The disability insurance payments you would want to receive each year if you or your husband became disabled $_____

Where Do We Go from Here?

After you've provided for self-insurance and emergencies (savings) and protection against financial loss from death or disability (insurance), you'll want to choose the long-term investments that will help you achieve the financial goals you listed on page 25.

In Section 15, financial planning in action, we deal with the specifics of financial planning: How much will you need when you retire? When will your children start college? What investments should you make for maximum after-tax yield?

Hold off choosing investments until you get to Section 15.

First, become familiar with the investment possibilities in Sections 5 through 10, beginning with Stocks and Bonds on page 59.

* You do not need 100% coverage because of preferential tax treatment given to people who receive disability insurance payments. Also, insurance companies do not provide 100% coverage.

Taking Stock of Stocks and Bonds

Stocks and bonds are the traditional investments most people use to provide income or make their money grow over long periods of time.

If you own *stock,* you have an *ownership* (equity) interest in a company, and share in the distribution of profits (dividends). *Bonds* are *debt* instruments issued by corporations and governments. If you own bonds, you are a creditor of the corporate or government issuer, and earn interest.

Companies Issue Two Kinds of Stock

Preferred stock pays a specific dividend (e.g., 10%) which is paid before any dividends are distributed to common stock owners. Some preferred stock issues may be exchanged for bonds or common stock under certain conditions.

Common stock pays no specific or guaranteed dividend. The amount of the dividend is set by a company's board of directors before each distribution.

Why Buy Stocks and Bonds?
Ten years ago, Helen and Charles started an investment program for their daughter's education with $2,000. They bought common stocks with the expectation that the stock would increase in value as the issuing companies prospered. Through judicious buying and selling and reinvestment of dividends in additional shares, Helen and Charles ac-

cumulated a fund large enough to cover the tuition bills that now arrive as regularly as the solstices twice a year.

Marsha, on the other hand, wanted additional income to supplement the salary she earns as a school teacher. With $5,000 to invest, she bought government bonds. They were safe and could be counted on to pay 12% interest, or $600, each year. Marsha knew she might earn a higher rate of interest on a corporate bond, or perhaps double her money on a "hot tip" in the stock market, but she felt she could not afford to risk losing any of the money she had taken so long to accumulate.

How Can You Be a Successful Investor?

- By being diligent and well informed.
- By buying securities that are appropriate for *your* financial goals.

The Risk-Return Trade-Off (see chart, page 61)

Because stock and bond prices go up and down, there is more risk of incurring a loss than there is with savings instruments (see Section 2). But there also is the prospect of a higher return.

NOTE: In general, the higher the *expected return on an investment the greater the possibility* of loss on that investment.

Usually, there is a positive relation between risk and return:

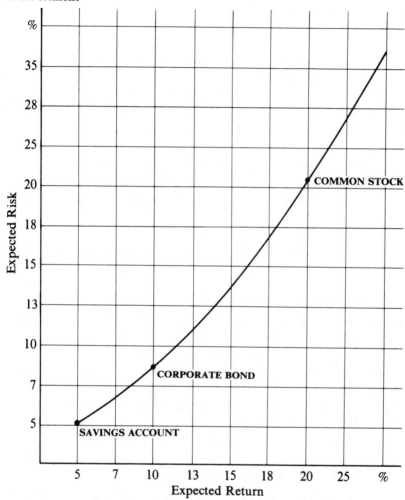

Everyone has her own tolerance level for risk. Ask yourself:

- If I lose money on an investment, will it affect my standard of living?

- If I make this investment, will I be able to sleep at night?

Only you can answer these questions, and they should be asked before every investment decision you make.

How to Pick a Stock

Choose an Industry with High Growth Potential
What are people buying or using in large amounts?

In what industries is supply limited relative to demand?

In what industries are technological developments making production of goods and services more efficient?

Look for the Leading Company in That Industry
Which company has brought out successful, new products? Which company has a reputation for being aggressive and innovative?

Look for Good Management
There is a high correlation between firms that are well managed and firms that make money for their shareholders.

Investigate the Company's Financial Status
If the company borrows (issues bonds or has bank loans), can interest payments be covered with current earnings?

What is the firm's *debt-equity ratio?* If the amount of capital contributed to the business by owner-shareholders is high, the D:E ratio is low. If the amount of capital borrowed is high, the D:E ratio will be high. The higher the D:E ratio, the higher the risk but also the higher the expected return on equity.

Are the company's earnings increasing every year?

Do You Want Income or Growth?

• *Income stocks:* Companies such as public utilities which pay high dividends; i.e., they distribute a large percentage of their earnings to shareholders.

• *Growth stocks:* Rapidly growing companies that "retain" (i.e., reinvest) the bulk of their earnings in the company and pay little or no dividends; a shareholder's return comes from expectations that the stock prices will rise as the company prospers.

Current income needs, risk tolerance, inflationary expectations and your tax bracket influence your investment decision.

How to Buy Stock as a Novice or with Limited Means*

1. Buy a few shares of stock in a company with high growth potential. Read its annual reports, interim reports, stockbroker research reports, newspaper and magazine articles. Attend the annual stockholders' meeting.

2. Participate in your employer's stock purchase plan. Some corporations provide stock options to their employees, which permit purchases at less than the market price of the company's stock.

3. Start an investment club with a group of friends. Each member makes a monthly contribution to the "investment kitty." Contact the local office of a large stockbrokerage firm to provide a broker for your club. The broker will attend your club's meetings and help you decide what stocks to buy.

For more information about investment clubs, write:
National Association of Investment Clubs
1515 East Eleven Mile Road
Royal Oak, Michigan 48067

4. Buy shares in a mutual fund. A mutual fund is an investment company which buys stock in many companies with money contributed to the fund by a large number of investors, and distributes profits earned by the fund to the investors. The investors own shares in the fund; the fund owns the securities.

Advantages of a Mutual Fund

- Permits investments of small sums of money ($25 to $2,500 initially; $10 to $100 subsequently).
- Professional management on the job every day.
- A diversified portfolio which means diversified risk.

* Financial institutions that sell stocks and bonds are listed on page 71.

- Shares bought in large quantities are purchased at a lower price and lower sales charge (commissions) than most individuals would pay.
- Investors are protected by stringent organizational requirements and continual supervision of mutual funds by the Securities and Exchange Commission (SEC).

Kinds of Mutual Funds: "Load" and "No-Load"

Load Funds
A sales charge is deducted from your initial investment.

EXAMPLE: You "invest" $1,000 *but* there is an 8% sales charge (the "load"). Therefore, your *actual* investment is $920.

No-Load Funds
No up-front sales charge. Fund management is compensated by a *management fee* which is a percentage of the average daily value of the fund's net assets. The fee is deducted from income paid to shareholders.

EXAMPLE:

Mutual fund earns 6%

Management fee .5%

Paid to shareholders: 5.5%

Kinds of Mutual Funds for Different Financial Objectives

Growth funds buy stocks expected to appreciate in value.

Income funds buy stocks that pay large dividends.

Mixed funds buy some stocks for growth and some for income.

NOTE: Buy mutual funds sponsored by large, well-capitalized, well-known brokerage firms or investment management companies.

For more information about mutual funds, write:
Investment Company Institute
1775 K Street, N.W.
Washington, D.C. 20006

How to Read the Stock Market Page

Stock's highest and lowest prices during preceding year

Price-Earning Ratio—Price = Preceding day's closing price per share

Earnings = Company's after-tax profits (funds available to pay dividends) per share.

A relatively high P:E ratio indicates expectation of stock's buyers of high future profits relative to other companies.

Example: If Dr. Pepper ("DrPepp")'s P:E ratio is 9, the preceding day's closing price might have been $12.50 and its earnings per share $1.40 (a 9:1 ratio).

Names of companies—"Walt Disney Products"
"Dow Chemical Corporation"

I.E. du Pont Common Stock
I.E. du Pont Preferred Stock

Annual *dividend* per share—
Duquesne Light is currently paying $1.90 per share, usually paid quarterly; in this example, 47½¢ per share per quarter.

Yield—Annual Dividend as percentage of previous day's closing price
($1.90 ÷ $13.38 = 14%)

The highest, lowest and final price per share at which the stock was purchased by investors during the preceding day.

52 Weeks High	Low	Stock	Div.	Yld %	P-E Ratio	Sales 100s	High	low	Close	Net Chg.
12⅝	10	DetEd	1.68	13.	6	321	12½	12⅜	12½	+ ⅛
61¼	48¼	DetE	pf5.50	9.1	..	4	60¼	60¼	60¼	−1
65	55⅝	DetE	pf9.32	15.	..	z720	62	61	61½	.....
53½	45	DetE	pf7.68	15.	..	z220	52	50⅛	51	+1
52	43⅛	DetE	pf7.45	15.	..	z450	50	49½	50	+ ½
22½	16¾	DE	pfF 2.75	14.	..	10	19	19	19	.....
22½	16½	DE	pfB 2.75	15.	..	3	18¾	18⅝	18¾	+ ⅜
16¼	13¼	DetE	pr2.28	15.	..	16	15⅛	14⅞	14⅞	.....
33	23¼	Dexter	1.10	4.2	10	55	26⅝	26	26⅜	+ ¼
14	8⅝	DiGior	.64	6.9	6	284	9¼	9⅛	9¼	+ ⅛
26¼	18⅜	DiGio	pf2.25	11.	..	52	19⅞	19⅝	19⅞	.....
46⅜	19	DialCp	1.40	2.9	12	47	u47¾	46⅜	47¾	+1¾
39⅜	26¼	DiaInt	2.20	6.0	15	66	36⅝	35¼	36⅝	+1⅛
39⅝	23¾	DiamS	1.76	6.3	8	843	28	27⅝	27⅞	− ⅛
48¼	31⅛	Diebd	s	..	16	24	46	45⅞	46	+ ¼
113¼	80¼	Digital		..	13	2151	91¾	90⅞	90⅞	−1⅛
13½	9⅞	Dilling	n .70	5.4	6	418	13	12¾	13	+ ⅛
25¾	13¼	Dillon	1.20b	4.8	10	28	25⅜	24¾	25⅛	+ ⅛
67⅛	43¾	Disney	1	1.8	15	746	54¾	54¼	54⅝	+ ⅛
6¼	2⅛	DivrsIn		..	6	127	2⅜	2¼	2¼	.....
15⅛	10¼	DrPepp	.80	6.4	9	734	12¾	12⅜	12½	− ⅜
26¾	15⅜	Dme g	s .16	..	..	529	17⅞	17⅜	17½	− ⅜
32⅜	20½	Donald	.66	3.1	8	77	21⅜	21	21¼	.....
14¼	7⅛	DonLJ	.20	1.4	12	343	14⅛	13⅞	14⅛	+ ¼
43	30⅛	Donnly	1.28	3.2	10	82	40⅝	40¼	40⅝	+ ½
31	16½	Dorsey	1	5.4	7	79	18¾	17¾	18½	+ ⅝
32⅜	24¼	Dover	s .66	2.2	12	547	29¾	29⅜	29⅝	+ ⅛
39	23¾	DowCh	1.80	6.7	8	6177	27⅛	26	26⅞	+ ¾
55¼	29	DowJn	s .92	1.7	25	126	53¼	52½	53	.....
31¾	15⅞	Dravo	s .96	5.6	9	198	17⅛	16⅞	17	+ ¼
57	30⅞	Dresr	.68	1.9	9	2900	37	34⅞	36¾	+2
16¼	13⅝	DrexB	1.99e	14.	..	27	14¾	14½	14½	− ½
29⅜	14⅛	Dreyfs	s.40a	1.5	8	46	27⅜	26¾	27	− ⅛
56	35¾	duPont	2.40	5.9	7	3064	41⅛	39⅞	40¾	+ ⅝
43	34	duPnt	pf4.50	12.	..	2	38¾	38¼	38¼	− ¼
22½	15½	DukeP	2.20	10.	7	499	22	21⅝	21⅝	− ⅜
90¼	65⅛	Duke	pf6.75	7.6	..	1	89⅜	89⅜	89⅜	− ⅞
66½	55	Duke	pf8.70	14.	..	z100	60⅛	60⅛	60⅛	−1⅜
64	52¾	Duke	pf8.20	14.	..	z3450	59	56¼	58¼	− ¾
59½	51	Duke	pf7.80	14.	..	z40	56½	56½	56½	.....
23	19⅛	Duke	pf2.69	13.	..	9	20½	20⅛	20¼	.....
66	55	Duk	pfM8.84	14.	..	z2700	62¼	62¼	62¼	+ ¼
62½	52⅛	Duke	pf8.28	14.	..	z200	59	59	59	+1
70¼	53¼	DunBr	2.36	3.6	16	102	64⅞	64¼	64⅞	+ ⅜
14⅛	11¾	DuqLt	1.90	14.	7	1570	13½	13¼	13⅜	− ⅛
18	14	Duq	pfA2.10	13.	..	z100	16⅛	16⅛	16⅛	− ⅝
14	11¼	Duq	pf 1.87	15.	..	z190	12½	12½	12½	+ ¼
15	12¼	Duq	pf 2	15.	..	z100	13½	13½	13½	.....
17	13¾	Duq	pr 2.31	16.	..	z700	15	14¾	14¾	.....
25	21⅝	Duq	pr 2.75	12.	..	z330	22½	22½	22½	.....
37	23⅛	DycoP	n.15e	.6	15	39	26¼	25¾	26¼	+ ¼
13	6¼	DynAm	.15	1.9	6	16	7⅞	7¾	7⅞	.....
		– E–E–E –								
47¾	32⅜	EGG	.64	1.5	19	358	42⅞	42	42⅜	− ⅝
55⅝	38⅝	E Sys	1	1.9	21	89	52¾	52¼	52¼	− ¾
22⅞	13⅝	EagleP	.96	7.2	6	971	13⅝	d13¼	13⅜	− ¼
28	15¾	Easco	1.32	5.8	7	14	22⅞	22⅝	22⅞	− ⅛
13⅛	6	EastAir		..	..	400	6⅜	6¼	6⅜	− ⅛
7½	2½	EAL	wtO	..	..	44	3⅛	3	3	.....
18⅜	14⅝	EsAir	pf2.69	17.	..	22	15¾	15½	15½	− ⅜
20¼	16¾	EsAir	pf3.20	17.	..	34	18¾	18⅝	18⅝	− ⅛
32	18	EastGF	1.20	4.8	11	544	25	24⅛	24⅞	+ ½
12½	10¼	EastUtl	1.60	14.	6	61	11¾	11½	11⅝	− ⅛
85⅜	60⅝	EsKod	3a	4.3	9	2202	70½	69⅛	70⅛	+ ¾
41½	25¼	Eaton	1.72	5.5	11	66	31⅜	31	31⅛	+ ⅛
57	42	Eaton	pf1.19	2.6	..	2	46	46	46	+ ½
14⅞	10	Echlin	.52	4.2	18	103	12⅜	11⅞	12¼	+ ¼
31¾	20⅛	Eckrd	s .92	3.7	11	1720	24⅞	24	24⅝	− ⅛
31¼	24	EdisBr	1.44	5.4	7	379	27	26⅞	26⅞	− ⅜
24	14½	Edwrd	s .60	2.6	8	155	23⅜	22⅞	22⅞	− ⅜
29½	19¼	ElPaso	1.48	6.0	10	324	24⅞	24½	24¾	.....
18⅝	15⅜	EPG	dpf2.35	14.	..	17	17¾	17⅜	17⅜	− ⅛
26⅛	22½	EPG	pf 3.75	15.	..	4	25⅜	25¼	25⅜	.....
19⅜	9½	Elcor	.30	2.8	90	24	11	10¾	10¾	− ¼
9⅜	4⅜	ElecAs		..	16	37	5¾	5½	5⅝	− ⅛
29⅝	14⅞	EDS	s .60	2.4	17	12	24½	24½	24½	− ⅛

Wall Street Journal, December 2, 1981

Bonds (see certificate, page 67)

Bonds are called fixed income securities because the issuer promises to pay the bondholder (bond owner) a fixed amount of interest for a specific time period.

The issuer also promises to repay principal (the amount of the bond) at the end of that period (on the due date or maturity date). The amount of the bond is also known as its face value.

Bonds usually are sold in $1,000 multiples, so $1,000 is the "par" price of a bond. If a bond's price falls below par, perhaps to $950, it is selling at a *discount*. If it rises above par, perhaps to $1,050, it is selling at a *premium*.

When bond prices are quoted by a bond broker or in the newspaper, the last zero of the price is left off. Par becomes 100, the discount price is 95, and the premium price is 105.

The price for which you sell a bond might be more or less than you paid for it.

Why Interest Rates and Bond Prices Change and Vary Inversely

September 1, 1981: Giant American Conglomerate Corporation (GAC) issued $50 million bonds in $1,000 units with a maturity date of 20 years. The *coupon rate* was 8%. This means that GAC promises to pay $80 per $1,000 per year to whomever owns the bond during those 20 years.

The coupon rate is determined by such factors as the maturity of the bond, GAC's credit rating (page seventy), and the current *yield* on bonds of lesser, similar or higher quality. The current yield of a bond is the relationship between its annual interest income and current market price. If the GAC bond sold for $1,000 on September 1, its current yield is the same as the coupon rate, 8%.

$$\frac{\text{Coupon Rate}}{\text{Market Price}} = \text{Current Yield} \quad \frac{\$80}{\$1,000} = 8\%$$

Although the coupon rate remains the same throughout the life of the bond, bond prices and current yields will change, and change in an

A Bond Certificate

$5,000 GIANT AMERICAN CONGLOMERATE CORPORATION $5,000

8% BOND DUE ON SEPTEMBER 1, 2001

Giant American Conglomerate Corporation promises

to pay to

JACQUELINE SMITH

8%

the sum of FIVE THOUSAND DOLLARS due 2001

on September 1, 2001, and to pay interest at the rate of 8% semiannually on March 1 and September 1 each year until the principal is paid. This bond is subject to redemption prior to its stated maturity date on or after March 1, 1991.

DATED: June 15, 1981   Giant American Conglomerate Corporation
FIRST NATIONAL BANK
Transfer Agent   PRESIDENT

Issuer

Registered owner of bond

Principal (amount of bond)

$80 per $1,000, annual interest (coupon rate)

$200 paid twice a year and sent to the registered owner.

The due date is the maturity date (this is a 20-year bond)

Some bonds may be redeemed or "called" before maturity. This bond has a 10-year "call protection."

Agent of the issuer, usually a bank responsible for making interest payments and redeeming bonds at maturity.

TAKING STOCK OF STOCKS AND BONDS

inverse relationship. As the bond price goes up, the current yield falls, and vice versa.

October 1, 1981: Because of inflationary expectations, an increase in the supply of bonds, a decline in the demand for bonds, or some combination of these factors, the 20-year bonds of the National Electronics Corporation (NEC) are issued to yield 8.5%. No prospective bond buyer will buy a GAC bond for $1,000 which pays $80 a year when she can buy a NEC bond that pays $85. Therefore, the GAC bond issued in September will sell in October for $941 in order to yield the same 8.5% as the NEC bond.

$$\frac{\text{Coupon Rate}}{\text{Market Price}} = \text{Current Yield} \quad \frac{\$80}{\$941} = 8.5\%$$

Because the *price* of the GAC bond has *fallen,* its *current yield* has *increased.** Anyone who bought a GAC bond on Sept. 1, and owns it on Oct. 1, is unaffected by the change in price and current yield. However, if she sold it on Oct. 1, she would have a capital loss of $59.00 ($1,000–$941).

December 1, 1981: Because inflationary expectations are lower, the supply of bonds has declined or the demand for bonds has increased, or some combination of these factors, the prices of GAC and NEC bonds have risen to $1,050 and the current yield has fallen to 7.6%:

$$\frac{\text{Coupon Rate}}{\text{Market Price}} = \text{Current Yield} \quad \frac{\$80}{\$1,050} = 7.6\%$$

Although the coupon, $80, remains the same throughout the life of the bond, bond prices and yields fluctuate in an inverse relationship. When bond prices go up, yields fall, and vice versa.

---

* The simple calculation of current yield is used to illustrate the inverse relationship between bond prices and yields. In fact, the *yield to maturity* (the income earned by a bondholder until a bond matures) will be greater than the current yield if a bond is purchased at a discount and lower than the current yield if a bond is purchased at a premium.

THE MONEY WORKBOOK FOR WOMEN

Who Issues Bonds?

The Federal Government (Governments)
These are the most creditworthy (lowest risk) bonds because they are issued by the U.S. Treasury or federal government agencies.

Government bonds with two- to ten-year maturities are called *notes.* Minimum investment: $5,000 for two to four years, $1,000 for four years or longer (Exceptions: Series EE and Series HH Savings Bonds.).

"Governments" with maturities longer than ten years are called *bonds.*

Minimum investment: $1,000 (not all issues).

NOTE: Flower bonds: Some low coupons (3–4½%) Treasury bonds may be purchased at a discount and used to pay federal estate taxes. Credit is given for the full face value of the bond. For example: $100,000 worth of flower bonds purchased for $80,000, will be accepted as full payment for a $100,000 estate tax bill.

Local and State Governments (Municipals)
Municipal bonds are known as tax-free bonds because the interest earned is exempt from federal income tax and exempt from state income tax in the state of issue.

NOTE: Formula to compare taxable with tax-free yields appears on page 71.

Municipals are issued for 1- to 40-year maturities.
Minimum investment: Usually $5,000.

Private Corporations
These bonds have higher yields than "governments" of comparable maturities.
Ten- to 40-year maturities.
Minimum investment: Usually $5,000.

NOTE: Bond mutual funds, offering the same features as stock mutual funds, are available for small investments.

Registered Versus Bearer Bonds

When you buy a bond, you may choose between having it registered or in bearer form.

A registered bond is registered in the name of the owner with the issuer's transfer agent (see bond certificate, page 67). A bearer bond, or "coupon" bond is not registered in any name. It belongs to the bearer, the person who has possession of the bond.

Owners of registered bonds automatically receive their interest payments twice a year from the transfer agent. Owners of bearer bonds must apply on each interest payment date for their interest payments. A coupon for each interest payment is attached to the side or bottom of a bearer bond certificate. On the interest payment date, the coupon is "clipped" and sealed in a special envelope provided by banks for their customers. The bond owner deposits the coupon in her account and the bank forwards it to the transfer agent for collection.

Bearer bonds are convenient when a bond is sold because they do not have to be returned to the transfer agent to be registered in the name of the new owner, but if they are lost or stolen, there is no record of ownership to protect the investor's property rights.

Choosing a High-Quality Bond

Most municipal and corporate bonds are rated by two independent credit rating agencies, Standard & Poor's and Moody's, for financial stability and ability to pay interest and principal to the bondholders. Both agencies use a letter-rating system to indicate relative quality:

STANDARD & POOR'S	MOODY'S
AAA	Aaa
AA	Aa
A	A
BBB	Baa
BB	Ba
B	B
CCC	Caa
CC	C
C	C

The first four ratings in each system are considered "investment grade" securities. Bonds become more speculative, and a higher risk to the investor, as their ratings descend toward "C."

All federal government securities are rated Triple A, the highest quality and least risky fixed income security.

How to Compare Taxable with Tax-Free Yields

FORMULA:

$$\frac{\text{Tax-free Yield}}{\text{(Your Tax Bracket)}} = \text{Equivalent Taxable Yield}$$

EXAMPLE: Assume: Municipal bond yielding 5%. You are in the 40% tax bracket.

$$\frac{5\%}{(1 - .40)} = \frac{5\%}{(.60)} = 8\%$$

You would have to earn *8%* on a U.S. government or corporate bond *on which you pay federal income tax* to earn the after-tax equivalent of *5%*.

Where to Buy Stocks and Bonds

The Federal Reserve Bank (12 District Offices and 15 Regional Offices)

Sells only new Treasury bills, notes and bonds. There is no service charge and you may pay by mail or in person. "The Fed" accepts personal checks. New issues are advertised in newspapers in advance of their sale dates.

Full-Service Stock Brokers

Offer a full range of investment services. They charge a commission or service charge on all security purchases and sales.

"Discount" Brokers

Are brokerage houses that transact only security purchases and sales. They have no investment management, advisory or research services. They usually charge lower commissions than full-service brokers.

Commercial Bank Customer Securities Departments

May buy and sell securities only at the customer's direction. Banks offer investment advice or investment management services other than in their trust departments. Bank service charges and commission may be more, less or the same as full service or discount brokers.

Shop around—stocks and bond sales charges vary.

EXAMPLE: $2,500 stock purchase (100 shares at $25 per share) September 11, 1981

	SERVICE CHARGE, COMMISSION OR COMBINATION—RANGE
Four Full-service Stockbrokers	$35.00—$64.00
Two Discount Brokers	$34.00—$45.00
Two Banks	$37.60—$47.60

Income Versus Growth

Your tax bracket, current income needs, risk tolerance and inflationary expectations should determine whether you invest for income (a known fixed rate of return) or growth (unknown but higher prospect of return).

Tax Considerations

One hundred percent of dividend and interest income is taxed as *ordinary income.* You pay the same tax rate on a dividend or interest payment as you pay on income earned from other sources, such as wages and salaries. Only 40% of a *capital gain,* the increase in value of a real or financial asset owned at least one year and a day, is taxed. (The tax is paid when the appreciated asset is sold.) Therefore, depending on your tax bracket, the *after*-tax return on a capital gain can be higher than the after-tax return earned from dividends or interest. See pages 141–143 for a full discussion of capital gains and losses.

EXAMPLE: You have $5,000 to invest. You have a choice between buying a bond issued by Giant American Conglomerate Corporation, paying annual interest of $500 (10%), or buying 100 shares of GAC's common stock which pay no dividend, but the price of which you expect will increase 10% during the coming year, from $50 to $55 a share.

Assume you are in the 30% tax bracket.

GAC BOND
Expected After-Tax Return

Annual interest	$500
less tax	150 (30% of $500)
After-tax return	$350
After-tax return	7%

GAC STOCK
Expected After-Tax Return

Capital gain	$500 (Difference between $5,000 and $5,500)
less	300 (60% of $500 not taxable)
	$200 (Taxable capital gain)

Capital gains tax (30% of $200) = $60
After-tax return ($500 − $60)   = $440
After-tax return   8.8%

Income Needs and Risk Tolerance

Although the *expected* after-tax return on the stock is higher than the *expected* after-tax return on the bond, the *probability* that GAC will pay 10% a year on the bond is greater than the *probability* that the price of the stock will rise 10%.

Individuals who want to earn current income and who have a low tolerance for risk usually prefer to buy fixed income securities and "income" stocks. Those who are willing to give up income in the present for the possibility of a higher return in the future and have a higher tolerance for risk usually prefer to buy "growth" stocks and other assets with potential for capital appreciation.

Inflationary Expectations

Between 1975 and 1981, the annual average rate of inflation (the rise in the Consumer Price Index) in the United States was 9%. During that period, the CPI varied from a low of 4.8% in 1976 to a high of 13.3% in 1979.

When inflation is expected to continue, investors try to protect their purchasing power (what they can buy with x number of dollars) by buying real and financial assets that increase in value, such as common stock and real estate, rather than financial assets with fixed values, such as savings instruments and bonds.

One of inflation's many negative side effects is the *paradox of risk:* People who can least afford to lose their savings, such as individuals near or past retirement age, feel they must make relatively high-risk investments with potential for capital appreciation in order to keep up with the rate of inflation.

Margin Accounts and Leaving Securities in Street Name

Margin Accounts

A *margin account* is a credit line at the stockbroker's. Customers who buy "on margin" (usually those making relatively large investments) borrow at interest rates comparable to bank loan rates to buy securities. The *margin* is the percentage of the purchase that the buyer must pay. For example, if the margin requirement is 75%, a customer would put up $3,750 on a $5,000 transaction.

The securities purchased are the broker's collateral. If the value of the securities declines before they are fully paid for or sold by the customer, the broker may call for additional "margin."

Leaving Securities in Street Name

Securities purchased by a customer but registered in a broker's name and kept by the broker are said to be held in *street name.* This is done for convenience by customers who buy and sell securities frequently and is required of those who purchase securities "on margin."

Some brokerage houses try to encourage customers who do not fall in these two categories to leave their securities in street name, ostensibly for safety and convenience. Although the securities belong to the customers, brokers may use these securities as collateral if they borrow from banks. This permits a firm to increase its working capital or provides funds which the firm lends at higher interest rates to margin account customers.

The primary drawback to leaving securities in street name is that all customer accounts are "frozen" if a brokerage house goes bankrupt. At best, securities held in street name will be distributed to their owners after a brief delay. If the securities cannot be returned, the Securities Investor Protection Corporation insures each customer's account for a maximum $500,000 loss, but it can take a year or longer for customers' claims to be filed and settled.

There's No Place Like Home

Can *you* afford to buy a house? One rule-of-thumb is that one month's housing expense (mortgage payment, real estate taxes, and homeowner's insurance) should be no more than one-quarter of your monthly income before taxes.*

For many people home ownership is a top priority financial goal. To see if you can afford to buy a home, fill out the following form:

Monthly income before taxes $＿＿＿＿＿

$$\times \; ¼ = \underline{\hspace{3cm}}$$

MONTHLY AFFORDABLE
HOUSING EXPENDITURE $＿＿＿＿＿

Purchase price of house	$＿＿＿＿＿	
less		
Down payment	$＿＿＿＿＿	
equals		
Mortgage	$＿＿＿＿＿	
Monthly repayment of principal & interest on mortgage† (__years at__%)		$＿＿＿＿＿
1/12 annual real estate taxes†		$＿＿＿＿＿
1/12 annual homeowner's insurance†		$＿＿＿＿＿
TOTAL MONTHLY HOUSING EXPENSES		$＿＿＿＿＿

* Lenders are required to take all sources of income into account in determining a prospective homebuyer's qualification for a mortgage (see page 40, If You Plan to Borrow. . .).

† Monthly mortgage payment information is available from realtors and lending institutions. A realtor or homeowner selling a house you want to buy should be able to tell you the current real estate taxes and homeowner's insurance carried.

Major Institutional and Other Sources of Home Financing

Commercial banks

Savings banks

Savings and loans associations

Credit unions

Mortgage companies

Realtors who have established relationships with financial institutions they deal with on a regular basis.

Builders of new homes who have a commitment for mortgage money from financial institutions they deal with.

When You Buy

• Make a *written* offer to the seller which includes the price you are willing to pay and a deadline for the seller's response. An *earnest money* deposit of $500 to $1,000 usually is required as evidence of the purchaser's sincerity.

• If your offer is accepted, you will sign an agreement of sale which)tates the closing date (when you will take possession of the property), and other terms of the sale. An additional earnest money deposit (usually bringing the total deposit to 10% of the purchase price) is required, which will be held in an escrow account and transferred to the seller on the closing date. *Request an interest-earning escrow account.* The income earned will be shared equally by the buyer and the seller.

• Make certain the agreement has a clause that says you are released from your obligation and get back your earnest money if you cannot get a mortgage within a specified period of time. The clause should include the maximum mortgage rate you are willing to pay.

• At the closing (also known as settlement), your money (the down payment) and the funds you've borrowed from the mortgage lender are transferred to the seller. The buyer also must pay *closing costs,* which include fees for title insurance (assurance that the seller has clear title to, and therefore the right to sell, the property) and a new property deed.

• Local property taxes usually are paid by homeowners once or twice a year. You have the option of paying taxes yourself when they come due *or* making pro-rated monthly payments to the mortgage holder who pays the taxes for you. In the second case, you are making payments before the funds must be transferred to the taxing authority. *Request an interest-earning escrow account* for the money put aside until the tax bill is due.

Different Kinds of Mortgages

The conventional mortgage with a fixed interest rate over the life of the mortgage is being supplemented or replaced by a variety of arrangements, some intended to make home ownership possible for people of limited means, others designed to induce lenders to make long-term commitments during times of scarce mortgage money and upward spiraling interest rates.

These alternatives to the conventional mortgage are not available in all geographic areas or from all mortgage lenders. They might be offered by state chartered lenders, but not federally chartered, or vice versa. They might be offered by savings institutions, but not commercial banks, or vice versa. Also, they may be *available* but not publicized, which means the burden is on the mortgage shopper to know about these alternatives and to *ask*.

Skip Payment Plan
Homeowner may "skip" five payments over the life of a mortgage; not more than one each year.

Graduated Payment Mortgage
Smaller payments during the early years, larger payments over the later years.

Balloon Mortgage
Variation of the graduated payment mortgage, with a large, or *balloon,* payment when mortgage is terminated.

Reverse Annuity Mortgage

Arrangement for older people to convert equity in their homes into a source of income. Mortgage lender makes monthly payments to the homeowner; homeowner builds up a mortgage obligation to the lender.

Variable Rate Mortgage

Interest rate moves up or down with changes in currently prevailing mortgage rates. Limit on amount and frequency variable rate can change.

Renegotiable Rate Mortgage

Variation of the variable rate mortgage. Fixed rate for three to five years; rate renegotiated for subsequent three- to five-year periods over the life of the mortgage.

Shared Appreciation Mortgage

Mortgage given at lower rate than currently prevailing mortgage rates, but homeowner must share appreciation in home's value with lender when property is sold.

Creative Financing

Purchase Money Mortgage

A home seller holds all or part of the mortgage obligation of the home buyer. This is intended as an inducement to buyer in tight money periods.

"Swing" Mortgage

A short-term loan used to buy a new house before a homeowner has received payment for her current residence which she has sold but not settled.

Real Life Monopoly: The Real Estate Investment Game

Q. What are the three characteristics of a good real estate investment?

A. Location, location and location.

If any investment is a "woman's investment," it seems to be real estate. We respond with a practiced eye to the features in a house or apartment that make it a desirable place to live. We mentally redecorate the pea-green wallpapered eyesore. We know instinctively that a fresh coat of paint and new fixtures will do wonders for a 30-year-old bathroom. And more than one real estate empire builder got her start driving around town while the kids were in school, checking out and comparing good buys.

When Mary and David decided to buy a house, Mary found a big old Victorian that had been divided into a two-family residence. A part of its appeal for her was that they could live on the first two floors, and the rent from the third-floor apartment would cover the mortgage. The other aspect of the house she liked was its location close to the city in a transitional suburban neighborhood. Mary saw other young people who could not afford expensive new housing being attracted by the spaciousness of the old properties, their gingerbread charm, and wide, tree-shaded streets.

Concerned about the prospect of costly major alterations, Mary and David bought the house only after being assured by a real estate appraiser that the house was structurally sound. They were able to keep their expenses down by doing painting, other cosmetic repairs and routine maintenance themselves. Each year they hired a professional contractor for one large renovation project, such as a new kitchen or restoration of the splendid oak parquet floors. They had no trouble finding a tenant and, as Mary had predicted, the house turned out to be an excellent investment. They enjoyed all the tax advantages of being landlords while they lived there, and sold the house after five years for twice the price they'd paid for it.

Why Buy Real Estate

Inflation Hedge

While the Consumer Price Index rose an average of 9% per year between 1975 and 1981, the value of a single family home rose an average of 12% annually.

Tax Advantages

Deductible expenses from federal income tax include:

Local real estate taxes

Interest on mortgage payments

Management and maintenance expenses

Depreciation (the dollar value of the amount a property is assumed to "wear out," or depreciate, each year)

Forty percent of any capital gains (increase in property's value when sold) is taxed at owner's highest tax rate

Leverage

Leverage is using borrowed funds on which you pay a fixed rate of tax-deductible interest to buy a property which you expect to increase in value.

EXAMPLE:

$60,000 property
$- 10,000$ down payment
$50,000 mortgage

Property sold in ten years for $100,000
Balance due on mortgage $40,000
$60,000 return on $10,000 = 60% per annum

Income

The rule-of-thumb used to be that you only bought rental properties that produced *net* rental income (after expenses) of at least 10% of the property's purchase price. High real estate prices and high mortgage rates have made 10% a difficult target to hit. Most people buy property today for the capital appreciation and tax benefits. However, it is possible for rental properties to become a good source of current income if annual rents go up faster than the rate of increase of carrying costs.

Choosing a Location for a Real Estate Investment

Best bet for the novice investor: A single home, two-unit dwelling or a condominium in your own geographic area. Buy in a community where the demand for rental housing is rising faster than the supply. Look for a region that's prosperous and expanding, or an inner city neighborhood being rehabilitated.

Buying far from home in a "hot" real estate market, such as parts of Florida, Texas and Arizona, is tempting but unwise for the small investor unless you have someone there to look out for your interest. Professional managers or rental agents charge 10 to 15% of gross rental income for their services.

Things to Think About Before You Buy

• Real estate is an illiquid investment (not easily or quickly converted to cash).

• The price at which you might have to sell could be lower than the price you paid. If you lose money on a real estate investment, will it affect your life style?

• If you don't have a tenant, can you afford to make monthly payments and maintain the property?

• Are you willing to take on the responsibilities of a landlady: renting the property, maintaining and supervising the property, etc.?

If You Lack the Means or Experience to Do-It-Yourself, Consider

• Buying shares in a real estate investment trust (RIET, pronounced *reet*).

A REIT is a mutual fund that builds or buys large real estate properties (apartment houses, office buildings) and distributes profits from rental income and property sales to the shareholders (called limited partners)

PROS:

professional management

diversification of holdings

tax benefits of individual ownership

reit shares available for a smaller investment than direct ownership would require

CONS:

REITs are highly leveraged (operate largely on funds borrowed from banks and insurance companies).

In a "down" market, REITs may not be able to attract enough tenants to generate the income needed to pay their debts.

• Starting a real estate investment club*

Get together a group of friends. Decide how much each woman should contribute (if there are ten women, $1,000 is a realistic minimum). Ask a real estate broker to advise your group and look for properties.

Have a partnership agreement drawn up by an attorney which states explicitly how to deal with such matters as cash deficits, the death or incapacity of a partner, and all other situations the partnership might confront.

Make allowance for an annual assessment of partners to pay for unanticipated repairs or other expenses.

---

* I first learned of the idea of women pooling their modest resources to buy real estate in 1974 when Louise Gilbert, a suburban Philadelphia realtor, organized Femme Sole. I am indebted to Louise for sharing the basic operating procedures of her group, and I am happy to report that Femme Sole has been a profitable, if at times harrowing, experience for its members.

How to calculate return on a real estate investment

Assume

$60,000 single house   ($450 monthly rental income)
$35,000 down payment
$1,000 settlement costs
Taxes: $800/year
Insurance: $400/year
Maintenance: $500/year
$25,000, 30-year mortgage at 12%   ($263 monthly payment)
20-year depreciation schedule
Property's market value will appreciate 10% each year, and that the property will be sold at the end of five years
Annual increases in rental income are offset by annual increases in taxes, insurance and other expenses

Annual cash flow

Rental income		$5,400
Less: Mortgage payments	$3,156	
Other expenses	1,700	
NET INCOME		$ 544

Annual taxable income

Rental income		$5,400
Less: Mortgage interest	$2,683	
Other expenses	1,700	
Depreciation	3,000	
TOTAL TAX DEDUCTIONS		7,383
TAX LOSS		($1,983)

Annual total return

Rental income		$5,400
Less: Mortgage payments	$3,156	
Other expenses	1,700	
NET INCOME		$ 544
Plus: Annual property appreciation—10%		6,000
TOTAL RETURN		$6,544

FIRST YEAR RETURN ON INVESTMENT $6,544 ÷ $36,000* = 18%

* $35,000 down-payment plus $1,000 settlement costs.

Return on investment if property is sold in five years

10% appreciation per year (compounded)	$96,631
Less: Balance on mortgage	− 22,000
TOTAL	$74,631
Less: down payment + settlement costs	36,000
CAPITAL GAIN	$38,631
Plus: $544 net income for five years	2,720
TOTAL PRE-TAX RETURN	$41,351

$$\frac{\$41,351}{\$36,000} = \frac{115\%}{5 \text{ years}} = 23\% \text{ gross return}$$

Calculating Capital Gains

40% of $38,631 gain is taxed according to personal tax bracket of property owner.

Assume: Property owner in 35% tax bracket

$$\begin{array}{r} \$38,631 \\ \times 40\% \\ \hline \$15,452 \text{ taxable income} \\ \times 35\% \\ \hline \$ 5,408 \text{ tax due} \end{array}$$

Total pre-tax return $41,351

Less: capital gains tax	− 5,408
NET RETURN	$35,943

$$\frac{\$35,943}{\$36,000} = \frac{100\%}{5 \text{ years}} = 20\% \text{ net annual return}$$

All That Glitters: Silver and Gold

People buy silver and gold for

- capital appreciation
- protection against inflation
- "insurance" against "doomsday"

Karen thinks that the demand for gold for ornamental and industrial uses will increase at a faster rate than the output of the world's gold mines will increase. She bought gold at $400 an ounce in 1981, and expects the price to be substantially higher when she sells it. If it is, she will pay the preferential capital gains tax on the appreciated value of her gold (see page one hundred sixty-three).

With prices rising every year, Diane believes she can better maintain the future purchasing power of her investment dollars with an asset like silver that has "intrinsic" (real) value than with assets denominated in depreciating dollars (savings instruments, stocks and bonds). Although the latter pay interest or dividends, and Diane earns no income on the silver coins she's bought, she expects the appreciated value of her real assets to more than make up for the loss of income she could earn on "paper" assets.

Vera is alarmed by the seemingly endless succession of international crises: territorial feuds, nationalistic crusades, military coups, civil wars, nuclear proliferation, *ad infinitum.* She fears a major economic or political catastrophe in the future that will make paper money worthless. She buys gold coins as her "insurance policy" for such a time when only precious metal has value as a medium of exchange.

You Should Buy Silver or Gold Only If:

• You can afford to lose all or part of your investment if you've got to sell at a lower price than the price at which you bought.

• You have a substantial portfolio of income-producing assets.

• You are, or intend to become, a diligent, knowledgeable collector of numismatic coins.

How to Buy Silver And Gold

Bullion

Bullion is a quantity designation for one troy ounce gold and one troy ounce silver.

Gold bullion coins—¼ ounce to 1–2 ounces.

Gold bullion "wafers"—1/20 ounce to 1 ounce.

Gold bullion bars—1 ounce to 400 ounces.

Silver bullion bars—1 ounce to 1,000 ounces.

NOTE: Prices reported in the newspapers and on daily radio and TV broadcasts are the New York Commodity Exchange (COMEX) prices for 100-ounce gold bars and 1,000-ounce silver bars. The price per ounce paid by purchasers is higher for smaller quantities.

BULLION COINS USED AS CURRENCY INCLUDE

GOLD	SILVER
South African Krugerrand	Pre-1965 U.S. nickels, dimes, quarters, half-dollars and dollars (sold in "bags" of $1,000 face value).
Canadian Maple Leaf	
Mexican Peso	
British Sovereign	
Austrian Corona and Ducat	
Hungarian Corona and Ducat	

NOTE: Dealers sell coins at a higher price (a "premium") than the daily quoted bullion price.

Numismatic Coins (Collectors' Coins)

Priced according to age, rarity, historic interest and artistic quality as well as *intrinsic* value (i.e., gold per ounce).

Since 1980, the U.S. Treasury has issued half-ounce and one ounce gold "medallions," coins minted as collectors' items rather than as currency. The price of the medallions is based on the prevailing market value of their gold content plus the costs of manufacture and distribution.

Jewelry and Commemorative Coins or Medallions

A silver bracelet or an engraved gold disk memorializing the 1976 Bicentennial are lovely to look at, but they are much less desirable investments than bullion and rare coins. You pay a mark-up over the value of the metal content for workmanship and the dealer's profit, and you'll sell for the wholesale price what you bought at the retail price.

Common Stocks

Common stocks are shares in silver- and gold-mining companies bought for prospect of capital appreciation *and* dividends.

Factors other than market price of the metal affecting value of shares:

Mine output and potential

Quality of mine management

Political environment (e.g., a political crisis in South Africa could affect gold production.)

Mutual Funds

Some investment companies hold only shares in silver- and gold-mining companies.

Gold Deposit Receipts or Certificates

This is a mutual fund concept; the organizing company buys a large quantity of gold. Participants are able to buy smaller quantities at a lower price than if they were making the purchases themselves. Certificates are issued to verify ownership.

Minimum initial investment: $5,000 to $25,000

Annual maintenance fee

Company may guarantee repurchase of units at a specified "premium" over the current market price

Where to Buy
Silver and Gold

Commercial banks	Stockbrokers
Currency dealers	Mutual fund organizations
Coin dealer coin "exchanges"	Jewelers

NOTE: U.S. gold medallions may be purchased by mail order from the Bureau of the Mint in San Francisco.

Remember

• You earn no interest on bullion or coins.

• The smaller the unit, the higher the price when buying and the lower the price when selling.

• In addition to the purchase price, you will pay a transactions fee (premium, commission or sales charge) and sales tax.

• You may have to pay shipping or storage charges.

• For security, silver and gold purchases should be kept in a safe deposit box and/or be insured.

• You will pay an *assay* fee (evaluation of metal's quality) when you sell.

• Get a written guarantee of your purchase's "fineness" (the proportion or amount of pure metal it contains).

• Comparison shop; prices, premiums and other charges vary.

Delectable Collectibles

ollectibles is a grab-bag word created to describe such assets as fine
rt, antiques, precious gems, stamps, coins and old books purchased
rimarily because they are expected to increase in value.

There always have been *collectors* who bought works of art for
heir beauty and quality, *antiquers* who haunt estate sales and junk
hops, and *hobbyists* for whom the satisfaction of knowing why a rare
tamp or coin was rare was as important as the acquisition itself. It is
nly in recent years that the combination of widespread affluence,
ouble-digit inflation and painfully high taxes have motivated large
umbers of people to invest in collectibles. Simultaneously, and in the
rue spirit of American enterprise, a large number of "investment op-
ortunities" have been created to meet every taste and pocketbook.

However, access to profitable collectible investing is not quite as
galitarian as collectible vendors want us to believe. Only professional
lealers, tenacious hobbyists and the wealthy have the time, money or
xpertise to "make a killing" in fine arts, precious gems, rare coins and
are stamps. Novice investors of modest means should concentrate on
ntique or "classic" furniture, *objets d'art* (everything from ceramic
himbles to leaded glass windows), old books, and items that evoke cu-
iosity or nostalgia for a historic period.

These are the "finds" that still turn up in thrift shops and musty
ld bookstores, at flea markets and yard sales. (The pros and the rich
re out there too, and on a more equal footing. In scavenging, the race
s to the swift.)

These kinds of collectibles are a particularly fertile field for
vomen. Many are everyday household items that homemakers are fa-

miliar with. A woman who enjoys bargain-hunting can learn to recognize a Queen Anne chair leg as easily as she recognizes a designer dress at Loehmann's. At night she can read *Antiques* magazine as well as *Better Homes and Gardens.* She and her friends can substitute no-calorie auction forays for weekday luncheons.

Successful collectible investors need not "love" the things they buy. They do need to be knowledgeable, persistent and lucky.

When You Buy Collectibles

All good collectible investments have four characteristics:

1. They are perceived to be the highest quality of their kind by experts in the field.

2. They are unique or in short supply relative to the demand for them.

3. They are nonliquid, i.e., they cannot be converted into cash quickly and easily.

4. They have high market risk, i.e., relative to other investments, there is a high probability that the price at which they are sold will be lower than the price at which they were purchased.

If you buy retail, choose a dealer who is well known in your community, recommended by someone whose opinion you value, and/or is a member of one of the following organizations:

Art: Art Dealers' Association of America

Antiques: National Association of Antique Dealers

Coins: Professional Numismatic Guild

Stamps: American Stamp Dealers' Association

Get a *written* description of your purchase and a guarantee of the item's authenticity from the seller. (Auction houses usually do not verify the authenticity of the collectibles they sell.)

Save your sales receipt or cancelled check. Verification of the date of purchase and the purchase price might be needed in the future.

Do not purchase collectibles through the mail "blind."

Check out newspaper, magazine and mail-order advertisers of collectibles. Write and ask for local references. Know *exactly* what you are getting *before* you pay for it. ("Investment-grade emeralds for $100 from South America" could be ten microscopic chips with no resale value.) Make certain there are no strings attached to a "money-back guarantee."

What Are Your Collectibles Worth?

A collection should be inventoried and appraised periodically. This is useful for tax purposes if the collector sells an item or dies, and for insurance claims if an item is lost or stolen.

Appraisals are done for a fee, and should be done by a qualified, reputable dealer who is a member of the American Society of Appraisers. The usual valuation standard is the most recent sale price of a comparable item.

If possible, attach photographs to your inventory. The possibility of precise identification might facilitate recovery if possessions are lost or stolen.

Collectibles Inventory

| | | | (date) |
DESCRIPTION	DATE OF PURCHASE	AMOUNT OF PURCHASE	CURRENT MARKET VALUE

DELECTABLE COLLECTIBLES

When You Sell
Collectibles

How to Sell

Privately through print advertising or at a house sale or flea market

Through a dealer

On consignment at an auction

REMEMBER:

Quick resale profits on collectibles are unlikely. They usually must be held at least three to five years for price appreciation that warrants the investment.

Collectibles held for more than one year are taxed when they are sold as long-term capital gains. There are no taxes on "paper" gains.

If you buy retail, you sell wholesale.

EXAMPLE:

Limited edition prints by the artist of the print you bought in 1976 for $200 are selling in 1982 for $400. You decide to sell your print back to the gallery. *Its buying price is $200, more or less what the artist receives before the gallery's mark-up.*

Tax Tips for
Collectible Investors

• The costs of appraising, insuring, mailing, storing and restoring collectibles are deductible expenses for the collectible investor (i.e., she who collects primarily to make a profit).

• If a collectible item is exchanged for another collectible item of like kind, no tax has to be paid on the appreciated value of the first item. However, the tax obligation is not entirely eliminated, but rather deferred until the second item is sold.

- If a collector gives a work of art that has increased in value to a nonprofit institution (e.g., museum, favorite charity, college alumnae association), she may deduct part or all of the appreciated value of the artwork from her taxable income. The amount of the deduction depends on whether the institution "uses the gift as part of its regular business" and whether the gift is retained or sold by the recipient.

- A collector who makes gifts from her collection during her lifetime will not have those collectibles included in her taxable estate when she dies *if* she does not retain a "present interest" in the gift. This means that the donee (person receiving the gift) must take immediate *possession* and *control* of the stamp collection, the Chippendale desk, the Imari plate, or whatever.

A Tax Shelter Is Not a Home

The best tax shelter is an economically sound business investment as well as a shelter.

The words *tax shelter* have a seductive appeal to anyone who wants to play the game of "more-for-me-and-less-for-Uncle-Sam." And talking about "my cattle herd" or "my oil well" certainly makes for more interesting cocktail party conversation than reporting on the ups and downs of a stock portfolio.

It's easy to understand why someone like Martha's husband Harold, a dentist who wants to give up his practice and retire to Florida, is attracted by such prospects as "200% depreciation" and "100% first year write-offs." The problem is that Harold hasn't the faintest notion how depreciation and write-offs will contribute to the income he needs in order to retire. Martha decides she had better find out.

What Martha learns is that any investment that offers the opportunity to reduce, defer or eliminate income taxes is a tax shelter. Municipal bonds "shelter" the income they pay (see Section 5). So do real estate investments (see Section 7) and government-regulated retirement plans (see Section 11).

However, the phrase *tax shelter* is used most frequently to describe certain kinds of large-scale projects in which participations are sold as "limited partnerships" (see next page). Some activities which are organized as tax shelters are oil and gas drilling, equipment leasing, farming, forestry, mineral excavation and real estate developments. The most recent entry on the tax shelter scene is a limited partnership organized to finance scientific and technical research and development.

The Federal Government offers a preferential tax policy for investment in these activities because they are considered relatively high risk and important for the country's economic welfare. If the projects are successful, investors are rewarded with higher *after-tax* income than they might expect to earn from other investments.

How Tax Shelters Organized as Limited Partnerships Work

Organization

The partners in a limited partnership are *investors*. They have no responsibility for or involvement in day-to-day administration and operations. It is a *limited* partnership because each partner's liability for the debts of the organization are limited to the amount he or she has invested.

The organizer of a limited partnership is the general partner.

The general partner receives a management fee and shares in income earned by the partnership. The general partner may or may not have invested in the partnership.

Profits and losses of the partnership are distributed in proportion to the ownership shares of each investor.

Participations in limited partnerships range from $2,500 per share to $100,000 or more.

There is no organized market for the purchase or sale of limited partnership shares. They are illiquid and may not be marketable. Some partnership agreements provide for the general partner to buy shares offered for sale by limited partners under certain circumstances.

Tax Benefits

Investors in a tax shelter are permitted to deduct real or "paper" losses generated by the project from their pre-tax income, thereby reducing taxable income and taxes. In some cases, they may take a tax credit which reduces owed taxes.

NOTE: The "at risk" rule: Since 1976, an investor's deductible losses are limited to the sum of the amount initially invested in the project plus any funds borrowed by the partnership for which the investor is personally liable; that is, the total monies the investor has *at risk*.

Expenses that Qualify as Tax Deductions or Write-Offs

- Depreciation of buildings and equipment
- Depletion allowance (oil and gas investments)
- "Intangible" drilling and development costs (oil and gas investments)
- Interest payments on loans and mortgages
- Maintenance and operating costs

Investment Tax Credit

A tax credit of up to 10% is pro-rated among partners for purchases of business equipment used in the production of income.

EXAMPLE:

A drilling rig is purchased for $200,000 by a limited partnership

10% tax credit $20,000

Partner Smith, who owns 5% of the partnership deducts her pro-rated share of the tax credit—$1,000—from the $15,000 in taxes she would have paid that year.

Partner Smith's federal tax bill is $14,000.

Capital Gains

The appreciation in the value of a capital asset owned by the partnership—an oil well, an office building, a cattle lot—is taxed when sold at the preferential capital gains rate: the individual partner's highest tax bracket times 40% (see page one hundred sixty-three).

EXAMPLE:

Initial investment $50,000

Sale proceeds $100,000

Capital gain $50,000

40% taxable share $20,000

An investor in the 50% tax bracket would pay $10,000 in taxes, or a real tax of 20% on the gain.

Caveats

Most tax shelters *defer* taxes. Deductions in the early years are offset by income taxed in later years.

After deductions reach the limit for which a limited partner is personally libel, the income generated by a tax shelter may not be adequate to cover income taxes and, if a partner has borrowed to invest in the shelter, interest payments.

Who Might Invest in a Tax Shelter

Taxpayers in the 50% tax bracket.

Taxpayers temporarily in a high tax bracket (e.g., actors, authors, sports stars); taxes can be deferred to a time when the taxpayer is in a lower tax bracket.

Investors who do not need liquidity. Most tax shelter programs run for five to ten years.

Investors able to tolerate the possible loss of their investment, financially and emotionally.

If You Plan to Buy a Tax Shelter

Have a lawyer, accountant or other professional who specializes in tax shelter investments evaluate a tax shelter you are considering. This should be a different person from the promoter of the tax shelter, who also may be a lawyer, accountant or tax shelter specialist.

Be Sure to Ask

• To have terms you do not understand explained in plain English. Most tax shelter prospectuses and promotional literature read as if they were written by a sadistic computer.

• How the shares in a limited partnership are allocated between the general partner and the limited partners.

• If the general partner has invested in the project.

- If the performance of previous projects organized by the general partner has been consistent with the original projections.

- For references from investors in the current or a previous project.

- Whether the shelter's tax losses can be offset against other income.

- What kind of tax deductions are offered (e.g., investment tax credit, depletion allowance), and how large the deductions are expected to be for each partnership share.

Remember:
The best tax shelter is an economically sound business investment as well as a shelter.

Investments in tax shelters should be consistent with your financial planning objectives.

Projections of tax savings and income are *expected,* not *guaranteed.*

Do not wait until the end of the year to buy a tax shelter.

Panic buying is unwise for all investments, but particularly so in the tax shelter area. There are more overpriced, low-quality tax shelters in December than snowflakes.

How to Enjoy Life After a Working Life

"From birth to 18, a girl needs good parents. From 18 to 35, she needs good looks; from 35 to 55, a good personality. After 55, hard cash."

—SOPHIE TUCKER

You need to plan for financial security in your old age if:
You work full-time for an employer with no retirement plan.

You work part-time and do not qualify for coverage under an employer's retirement plan.

You might not be employed by the same employer long enough to qualify for retirement benefits.

You could not maintain a comfortable life style on company retirement benefits, Social Security benefits, or both.

Your family's income would be drastically reduced by the death or disability of a working husband.

Your husband should die without a will and part of the assets you would have inherited are distributed by the state to other heirs.

Your working husband's company retirement plan has no survivor benefits.

Your retired husband's retirement plan has no, or reduced, survivor benefits.

You were divorced and your ex-husband couldn't or wouldn't provide adequate income and/or assets for you to maintain the life style to which you are accustomed.

You were divorced at an age too late to find remunerative employment and too soon to receive the benefits Social Security provides to the ex-wives of retired workers.

You expect to receive an inheritance or you have an affluent, generous husband, but you know that nobody looks out for your interest as well as you do yourself.

How much will you need to retire?*

			EXAMPLE
Current age _____			40
Retirement at age _____			65
Retirement in _____ years			25
Desired income per year during retirement years $_____†			$50,000
Sources of retirement income:			
Social Security benefits	$_____	/year**	$10,000/year
Company retirement plan	$_____	/year††	$10,000/year
Total expected retirement benefits	$_____	/year	$20,000/year
Additional income needed to reach desired income goal	$_____	/year	$30,000/year

What **lump sum,** *earning* X *rate of interest per year, will give you the additional income you want each year during your retirement?*

Assume an annual rate of return of	_____ %		6 %	
Divide: Desired additional income per year	$_____ (1)			
Divided by			$ 30,000	
Assumed annual rate of return and multiply by 1000	_____ % (2)		6	%
Equals				

---

* Homemakers can plan with their husbands *or* for their own post-65 financial independence.

† Desired retirement income should be less than pre-retirement income because work-related expenses are eliminated, *but* inflation must be taken into account, *so* choose a *realistic* amount that you think would support a comfortable retirement life style.

** Currently, the maximum benefits paid to women, whether they are retired workers or homemakers, is $9,000.

†† Employee must be employed at time of retirement to receive projected retirement plan benefits.

Lump sum that must be accumulated
   to earn the additional income $_____ (3) $500,000

Check: __ % (2) × $_____   (3) = $_____

                               6% × $500,000 = $30,000

How much will you need to save or invest each year to have that lump sum accumulated by the time you retire?

			EXAMPLE
Lump sum that must be accumulated	$_____	(3)	$500,000
Deduct: Income-producing assets (savings,	$_____		$ 5,000 savings
stocks,	$_____		$ 20,000 stocks
bonds, etc.) currently owned:	$_____		$ 10,000 bonds
TOTAL	$_____		$ 35,000
Additional amount that must be accumulated	$_____	(4)	$465,000

Turn to Accumulation Table (page 118)

Find the *row* that corresponds to the rate
of interest you think you could earn each
year on your investments during the accumulation period   _____ %   8 %

Find the *column* of years that corresponds
to the number of years until you plan to
retire   _____ years   25 years

Divide the additional amount you need to
accumulate during those years (4) by the
amount at the *intersection* of the above row
and column (5) and multiply by $1,000 $_____ (4) = $465,000 =
                                            $_____ (5) $ 78,954

This is how much you need to set aside
each year and earn a rate of __% per
annum to accumulate an additional
$_____ by the time you retire in __
years $_____ $ 5,890

What You Should Know About Your Company's Retirement Plan

• Age or years of employment before you are "vested" (begin to qualify for retirement benefits)

_____
(years or age)

• Age or years of employment to receive 100% retirement benefits

_____
(years or age)

• Minimum age at which you may receive a pension and how much you will receive

_____
(minimum age)   (benefits at minimum age)

• Whether there is a mandatory or "normal" retirement age

_____
(mandatory or normal retirement age)

• The formula the company uses to calculate the dollar amount of your pension

_____
(how pension is calculated)

• Whether the company's calculation includes Social Security benefits

Yes ☐   No ☐
_____
(includes Social Security benefits)

• Whether an employee may make voluntary contributions to the pension fund, and if so, how much

Yes ☐   No ☐
_____
(voluntary contributions permitted)

_____
(amount or % voluntary contributions)

• Whether you have the option of receiving your pension as a lump sum distribution (all at once) or paid out in regular installments over a specified period of time

Yes ☐   No ☐
_____
(lump sum or pay-out option)

_____
(option chosen)

• That there may be tax advantages or disadvantages associated with a lump sum distribution or installment pay-outs, depending on your tax bracket when you retire

- Whether and how you are covered by the company plan if there is a "break in service" (e.g., temporary layoff by employer, disability leave, leave of absence)

Yes ☐ No ☐ _____

(covered during break in service)

- You may name anyone you wish as your beneficiary or beneficiaries to receive the current value of your retirement benefits upon your death

_____

(beneficiaries)

- Whether the spouse of an employee may collect all or part of the employee's accumulated benefits if the employee dies before retirement

Yes ☐ No ☐ _____

(survivor's benefits pre-retirement)

- Whether the spouse of a deceased retired employee continues to receive retirement benefits, how much, and for how long

Yes ☐ No ☐ _____

(survivor's benefits post-retirement)

- Whether a surviving spouse has the option of taking death benefits as a lump sum or in periodic installments

Yes ☐ No ☐ _____

(lump sum or pay-out option)

- That there may be tax advantages or disadvantages associated with a lump sum distribution or installment pay out, depending upon the size of the decedent's estate and tax bracket

_____

(option chosen)

- That a surviving spouse has the option of "rolling over" a distribution received as a beneficiary into a nontaxable Individual Retirement Account (IRA)

- If you leave the company before your "normal" or mandatory retirement date, what portion of the value of your pension fund earned to date, if any, you will receive

_____

(termination benefit)

- If you can no longer work because you are permanently and totally disabled, whether you are entitled to the value of your pension earned to date

_____

(disability benefit)

- If you are vested and leave a company, you may "roll over" the distribution you receive into an IRA and not pay taxes on the distribution, even if you become self-employed or go to work for another company with a retirement plan

- That you may "roll over" the distribution you receive from one employer's retirement plan into another employer's retirement plan if the second employer is willing to accept it

- Whether you may borrow from the pension fund for such purposes as your children's education, a home purchase or medical expenses

Yes ☐ No ☐
(loan benefit)

- That you should receive a summary of the plan's annual financial report and the amount of your vested interest, once a year

Yes ☐ No ☐
(receive financial report)

- That employer contributions to retirement plans and the income earned on those contributions are exempt from income taxes. The distribution received by an employee or the employee's beneficiaries is taxable unless the distribution is "rolled over" into an IRA within a specified time period

---

Do-it-yourself Retirement Plans

Individual Retirement Accounts (IRAs)
Keogh plans
Annuities

BASIC CONCEPTS AND ADVANTAGES:

1. **You do not pay taxes on funds placed in an IRA or Keogh the year you make a "contribution."***

---

*See page 114 for tax treatment of contributions to annuities.

EXAMPLE:

Annual Salary	$25,000
Retirement plan contribution	1,000
Taxable income (before other deductions)	$24,000

2. **You do not pay taxes on income earned by the investments in a retirement plan, permitting faster growth of your retirement fund than if the income were not tax-sheltered.**

EXAMPLE:

Investment income earned by retirement plan—year 1	$500
Income available for reinvestment—year 2	$500

VS.

"Nonsheltered" investment income earned—year 1	$500
Income available for reinvestment year 2 (assume 30% tax rate)	$350

3. **Taxes must be paid on income withdrawn from a retirement plan, but because many workers are in a lower tax bracket in their retirement years than they were in their income-earning years, the tax paid is lower.**

EXAMPLE:

"Nonsheltered" investment income earned during income-earning year	$100
Net (after-tax) income (assume 40% tax rate)	$ 60

VS.

Income withdrawn from retirement fund during retirement year	$100
Net (after-tax) income (assume 24% tax rate)	$ 76

What You Should Know About Individual Retirement Accounts

Who May Have an IRA

1981: Workers not covered by a company retirement plan

After 1981: *Anyone whose income comes from wages or salaries, whether or not covered by a company retirement plan*

1981: Self-employed individuals, even those who do part-time work at home

After 1981: *Self-employed individuals, even those who have a Keogh plan* (see page 113)

Homemakers whose spouses agree to set up an IRA for the two of them

An employee whose employment has been terminated, or company plan has been terminated, may "roll over" the distribution received from the plan into an IRA

A spouse who receives a lump sum distribution from a deceased spouse's company retirement plan

NOTE: Excluded from eligibility for an IRA is the *nonsalaried homemaker,* the woman whose "income" comes from her household money, alimony or child support and who has no working spouse willing to set up an IRA. Her need for old age financial security certainly is as great as the individuals who do qualify.

If you want nonsalaried homemakers to be eligible for IRAs, write to your representatives in Congress and the Chairman of the Committee on Ways and Means, House of Representatives, 1102 Longworth House Office Building, Washington, D.C. 20515

How Much May Be Contributed to an IRA

1981: 15% of gross annual income or a maximum of $1,500 each year. After 1981: *100% of earned income with a maximum of $2,000.*

EXCEPTIONS:

1. 1981: Workers who establish spousal IRA's may contribute a maximum of $1,750 a year to two accounts. After 1981: *The maximum increases to $2,250, divided any way the spouses choose, so long as neither account has more than $2,000.*

2. The whole lump sum distribution received may be contributed to a "roll-over" IRA.

3. Simplified Employee Pension Plans (IRA's funded by an employer for each eligible employee) permit a maximum annual contribution of $7,500 to each account.

How, Where and When to Open an IRA

Commercial banks, savings institutions, insurance companies, brokerage firms, mutual funds, and trust companies act as "trustees" for IRA's. They maintain records of your annual contributions and earnings, and invest at your direction.

An IRA may be invested in a wide range of assets: savings certificates, annuities, stocks, bonds, mutual funds. However, some institutions, such as banks and insurance companies, permit purchases only of the investment vehicles they provide, such as savings instruments or annuities.

Mutual funds, brokerage firms, and trust companies offer more investment diversity and flexibility. For example, an IRA with a mutual fund company permits monies to be shifted among different kinds of funds (money market, equity, bond, etc.) managed by the company with no fee and no restriction on the frequency of these changes. Mutual fund companies charge a nominal fee to open an IRA and a small, annual management fee. Brokerage firms also charge a fee to open an IRA, and an annual management fee in addition to the commissions charged on the purchase and sale of securities. Trust companies charge an annual management fee, plus fees for account openings, account terminations and security transactions.

You may change institutional trustees *once a year* without penalty, so long as the change is made within 60 days of the termination of the original account.

An IRA for 1981 may be opened until April 15, 1982.

After 1981, employees covered by a company retirement plan may make tax-deductible contributions to the plan up to the allowable $2,000 maximum. These voluntary contributions are pooled and invested with the employer's contributions, but are otherwise subject to the same terms regulating IRA's.

Age at Which an Account Holder May Make Withdrawals from an IRA

You may begin to make withdrawals from an IRA when you are 59½ years old, and *must* begin to withdraw from the account when you are 70½ years old.

If withdrawals are made prior to age 59½, there is a 10% excise tax penalty plus regular income tax due on the amount withdrawn.

If the account holder becomes totally disabled, there is no penalty tax on a pre-59½ distribution.

Distribution Options

- *Lump Sum*—total contributions and reinvested income withdrawn at one time.

- *Installment Pay outs:*

  for a specified period of time

  for the account holder's lifetime

  over the life of the account holder and spouse

Tax Consequences of Distribution Options

A lump sum distribution is taxed during the year of the distribution or on the basis of five-year income averaging. (see "Income Averaging," page 141)

Distributions paid periodically from an IRA are taxed during the year the payments are made. Funds remaining in the account are not taxed until they are withdrawn.

Death and Taxes

A deceased account holder's IRA is not subject to *estate* taxes if the proceeds of an account are distributed to the account's beneficiaries over a period of 36 months or more.

A beneficiary pays *income* tax on a distribution from an IRA during the year the distribution is received.

There are neither estate taxes nor income taxes on a lump sum distribution from a company retirement plan if the distribution is "rolled over" into an IRA for a surviving spouse.

What You Should Know About Keogh Plans

Who May Have a Keogh Plan

- Full-time or part-time self-employed individuals.
- Business partnerships.
- Professionals such as doctors, lawyers, and accountants.
- "Moonlighters" who also may be covered by a company retirement plan.

NOTE: Employees of an employer who has a Keogh plan must be included in the plan if they work full-time and have been employed by the employer for three years or more.

How Much May Be Contributed to a Keogh Plan

1981: 15% of gross annual income or a maximum of $7,500 each year.

After 1981: *15% of gross annual income or a maximum of $15,000 each year.*

The percentage of income contributed to the plan for employees must be the same as the percentage contributed for employers.

If there is at least one employee, an employer and employees may make voluntary contributions with after-tax dollars of 10% of their annual income, with a $2,500 maximum for employers.

How, Where and When to Open a Keogh Plan

See "How, Where and When to open an IRA," pages 111 through 112.

Age at Which a Participant May Make Withdrawals from a Keogh Plan

Employers may begin to make withdrawals from a Keogh Plan at 59½ years old, and *must* begin to withdraw from the account at 70½ years old.

If withdrawals are made prior to age 59½, there is a 10% excise tax penalty plus regular income tax due on the amount withdrawn.

Employees may make withdrawals upon retirement or termination of employment at any age.

There is no penalty for withdrawal of voluntary contributions from the plan by employers or employees.

If a plan participant becomes totally disabled, the participant's total share may be withdrawn at that time.

Distribution Options

Same as for IRA; see page 112.

Tax Consequences of Distribution Options

A lump sum distribution is taxed as ordinary income during the year of the distribution or on the basis of "ten-year income averaging."

Distributions paid periodically from a Keogh plan are taxed as ordinary income during the year the payments are made. Funds remaining in the account are not taxed until they are withdrawn.

Death and Taxes

Same as for IRA; 112.

What You Should Know About Annuities

An annuity is a guaranteed income plan purchased from a life insurance company. Annuities are frequently, but not always, purchased to provide retirement income. An employer or worker makes contributions to the annuity during the working years, and income is paid periodically from the annuity to the worker (the annuitant) during the post-working years.

Different Kinds of Annuities

Annuities Purchased with Pre-Tax Dollars

Purchased by participants in IRA's, Keogh plans, and employees of public school systems and nonprofit organizations.

Annuities Purchased with After-Tax Dollars

Defer taxes on the income earned until income is paid to the annuitant.

Fixed Premium Annuity
The same contribution is made periodically throughout the accumulation period (e.g., $100 a month, $1,000 a year).

Variable Premium Annuity
The participant has the option to make periodic contributions of different amounts during the accumulation period (e.g., $1,500 one year, $2,000 the next).

Single Premium Annuity
A lump sum contribution, such as $10,000 or more; frequently purchased with proceeds received by the beneficiary of an insurance policy or pension fund.

Immediate Annuity
Income distributions to the annuitant begin immediately; usually a single premium annuity.

Deferred Annuity
Income distributions begin a number of years in the future as specified in the annuity contract.

Single Payment Annuity
A lump sum distribution of accumulated contributions and income earned by the annuity.

Fixed Payment Annuity
A guarantee that a specific minimum income will be paid periodically for a specific number of years or throughout the annuitant's lifetime.

Variable Payment Annuity
Fixed premium paid; income payments guaranteed for a specific number of years or throughout the annuitant's lifetime, but the amount of each payment varies according to the income earned by investments (usually common stocks) in the annuity's portfolio.

Joint and Last Survivor Annuity
A fixed payment annuity for two or more persons; amount of payments are reduced after the death of one of the annuitants.

Joint Annuity

Payments terminate after the death of one of two annuitants.

How Much May Be Contributed to an Annuity?

Annuities purchased for IRA's and Keogh plans are subject to the same annual limitations as other investments purchased for these accounts (see pages 110 and 113).

Employees of public school systems and nonprofit organizations may contribute as much as 20% of their gross income annually if they are not covered by an employer's retirement plan, and the difference between 20% and the percentage of income contributed by their employer if they are covered by an employer's retirement plan. The amount of the contribution is deducted from taxable income.

There is no maximum on contributions to annuities purchased with after-tax dollars.

Minimum contributions are determined by the policy of each insurance company (e.g., $10/month, $1,000/year for fixed and variable premium annuities; $10,000 for a single payment annuity).

If You Are in the Market for an Annuity

Sales charges, investment performance, guaranteed yields, estimated yields, and actual yields vary greatly among annuities. Shop around. Ask: "If I invest x amount each year for x years, how much will I have accumulated in my account x years from now? What will my monthly income be for x years, for life, for the lifetime of me and my spouse?"

The amount of money actually invested on your behalf may be less than the amount of money you gave the insurance company to invest because of the sales charge, or "front-load," on each premium you pay.

EXAMPLE:

Annual premium	$1,000
8% sales charge	− 80
Amount invested	$ 920

Sales charges can reduce or eliminate an annuity's tax advantages compared with non-tax-sheltered investments.

Charges for management fees and other expenses also may be deducted from your premiums.

Insurance companies project "estimated" yields and low "guaranteed" yields for their annuities. The actual income you receive might be more than the guaranteed rate, but the only rate an annuitant can depend on is the guaranteed rate.

You can withdraw the accumulated cash value from an annuity at any time, but the amount you receive might be less than the amount of premiums you paid. There also can be a "termination" charge deducted from the proceeds, calculated as a percentage of the proceeds ("rear-load") or as a flat rate (e.g., $25).

Either the *amount* being paid out or the *time period* over which payments are made can be guaranteed by the insurance company.

Withdrawals of principal from annuities purchased with after-tax dollars are not taxed unless the amount withdrawn exceeds the amount of the premiums paid in.

Annuity payments are taxed as ordinary income in the year payments are made.

An annuitant who elects the monthly income payments distribution option may not stop the payments and receive a lump sum distribution once payment begins.

If the death benefits of an annuity are payable to a beneficiary as an annuity, no estate taxes are paid and payments are taxed as ordinary income.

If death benefits of an annuity are payable as a lump sum, estate taxes must be paid but favorable income-averaging can reduce income taxes.

Accumulation Table

Dollar amounts indicate accumulation at end of specific time periods of $1,000 invested each year at different compound rates of interest.

Time Period

Rate of Interest	5 years	10 years	15 years	20 years	25 years	30 years	35 years	40 years
5	5,802	13,207	22,657	34,719	50,113	69,761	94,836	126,840
5½	5,889	13,584	23,641	36,786	53,966	76,419	105,765	144,119
6	5,975	13,972	24,673	38,993	58,156	83,802	118,121	164,048
6½	6,064	14,372	25,754	41,349	62,715	91,989	132,097	187,048
7	6,153	14,784	26,888	43,865	67,676	101,073	147,913	213,610
7½	6,244	15,208	28,077	46,553	73,076	111,154	165,820	244,301
8	6,336	15,645	29,324	49,423	78,954	122,346	186,102	279,781
8½	6,429	16,096	30,632	52,489	85,355	134,773	209,081	320,816
9	6,523	16,560	32,003	55,765	92,324	148,575	235,125	368,292
9½	6,619	17,039	33,442	59,264	99,914	163,908	264,649	423,239
10	6,716	17,531	34,950	63,002	108,182	180,943	298,127	486,852
11	6,913	18,561	38,190	71,265	126,999	220,913	379,164	645,827
12	7,115	19,655	41,753	80,699	149,334	270,293	483,463	859,142
13	7,323	20,814	45,672	91,470	175,850	331,315	617,749	1,145,486
14	7,536	22,045	49,980	103,768	207,333	406,737	790,673	1,529,909
15	7,754	23,349	54,717	117,810	244,712	499,957	1,013,346	2,045,954
20	8,930	31,150	86,442	224,026	566,377	1,418,258	3,538,009	8,812,629

EXAMPLE: $1,000 invested at 8% each year for 10 years would be worth $15,645 at the end of that time period. $1,500 invested at 8% each year for 10 years would be worth $23,468.

Who Owns What: While You're Here and After You've Gone

Estate planning means organizing your financial affairs so that after you've enjoyed the use of your possessions during your lifetime, they go to whom you want, in the manner you want, depleted as little as possible by taxes and other expenses. It includes gifts made *during* your *lifetime* as well as bequests distributed through a *will.*

Everyone should have a will. The purpose of having a will is to control the disposition of your property. If you die without a will (intestate), your assets are distributed by the *state,* and *not necessarily to whom you would want.*

Like many people, Sam never got around to writing a will. He assumed that his wife, as his closest relative, would inherit his property whether he had a will or not. In fact, when Sam died, the laws of the state of Pennsylvania directed that his wife receive only $20,000 plus one-half of the balance of his $100,000 estate. The remaining $40,000 was given to their young children, with a court-appointed guardian to look after the children's share. Sam's wife had to consult with the guardian about everything from their daughter's piano lessons to their son's orthodontist.

Also, since he hadn't written a will, Sam hadn't appointed an *executor* for his estate either. Therefore, the court had to appoint an *administrator* for Sam's estate, for whom a bond had to be posted. This created an additional expense for the family, and delayed the distribution of Sam's property to his wife and children.

Joint ownership of property is not a satisfactory substitute for a will.

Do you have a will?   YES ☐ NO ☐

When was it written: _____
(year)

Have your personal or financial
circumstances changed since then?   YES ☐ NO ☐

NOTE: All wills should be reviewed, and rewritten if necessary, to take into account changes in estate and gift tax laws made by the 1981 Tax Act.

If you don't have a will, or if your old will needs updating, make an appointment with a lawyer as soon as possible.

Because a lawyer's time is expensive, go prepared with the following information:

Checklist for Preparing A Will

The names of your executors and second choices if the executors can't or won't serve

_____

_____

_____

Whom you want to inherit your assets

_____

_____

_____

What you want each beneficiary to receive

_____

_____

_____

How your business or professional practice should be disposed of

_____

_____

_____

The *timing* of property transfers: immediately, over a period of time, or in the future

_____

_____

_____

Whether there should be *outright distributions* or assets should be held in trust

_____

_____

_____

Take along a copy of your Personal Financial Inventory (Section 1) to give the attorney a complete picture of your current financial situation.

Who Might or Should Be an Executor

Because of the many details and complexities associated with estate administration, you might want to name an experienced professional, such as a lawyer or accountant, or an institution, such as a bank trust department, as executor of your estate. A family member could serve as co-executor.

"Outside" executors charge a fee for their services, but the amount of the fee can more than offset the alternative cost of inept management by an inexperienced or unknowledgeable relative.

Whoever serves as executor, the services of an attorney for the estate also may be required. This can be your family lawyer, but an attorney who specializes in estate and tax law should be hired for large, complex estates.

Before you make a commitment, ask "outside" executors and lawyers how they charge for their services (flat fee, hourly charge, or percentage of estate's value) and ask them to give you a written estimate of what the fee will be.

If You Are Named As Executor in a Will

Your job *generally* is to gather together the decedent's assets, pay the estate's debts and taxes, and distribute bequests to the decedent's heirs. *Specifically,* you are responsible for some or all of the following:

- Locating the decedent's last will.

- Appointing an attorney as counsel for the estate if needed and the decedent had not done so.

- Filing the will for probate (official appointment of executor and confirmation before a local authority, such as the Register of Wills, that will is the decedent's last will).

- Acquiring copies of the death certificate as confirmation of death for banks, insurance companies, Social Security claims, etc.

- Filing claims for and collecting life insurance proceeds payable to the estate or other beneficiaries.

- Locating and making an inventory of all the decedent's assets, including contents of safe deposit boxes.

- Listing all the decedent's liabilities and verifying the validity of claims presented for payment.

- Closing decedent's bank and brokerage accounts.

- Opening a checking account for the estate.

- Maintaining records of all income earned by the estate before assets are distributed.

- Investing income earned by the estate in short-term interest-earning assets (savings account, money market fund, etc.).

- Determining the value of all assets as of the date of the decedent's death.

- Arranging for appraisals of real estate and personal property.

- Selling assets to raise funds for payment of debts and taxes.

- Collecting debts owed the decedent.

- Notifying beneficiaries of their bequests.

- Determining the appropriate time to make distributions to beneficiaries.

- Arranging for the preparation of federal and state death tax returns and income tax returns.

- Paying the federal estate tax within nine months of decedent's death, and state estate or inheritance taxes, if any, when due.

- Paying federal and state income taxes when due.

- Arranging for preparation of a final accounting of the estate for the appropriate authorities.

Estate, Inheritance and Gift Taxes

Federal Estate Tax
Levied on the current market value of all assets owned by an individual at her (his) death, *less* estate administrative expenses, burial and final illness expenses, debts, bequests to a spouse and charitable bequests.

State Estate Tax
Imposed by some states; computed on the basis of the maximum federal credit allowed for state death taxes.

Inheritance Tax
Imposed by some states on bequests made by a decedent in his or her will; the amount of the tax may vary according to the beneficiary's relationship to the decedent.

Federal Gift Tax
A tax on the transfer of property during one's lifetime; usually paid by the donor.

State Gift Tax
Imposed by some states; amount of tax may vary according to the recipient's relationship to the donor.

No income tax is payable on gifts or inheritances.

Who Pays Estate and Gift Taxes

Unified Estate and Gift Tax

Since 1976, a single tax schedule, called the Unified Estate and Gift Tax, has been applied to some gifts made during one's lifetime and to all bequests designated for after one's death.* Before 1976, life-

* See page 124 for tax-free lifetime gifts.

time gifts were taxed at a lower rate than testamentary (after-death) gifts.

The 1981 Tax Act increased the amount of lifetime and testamentary gifts that may be made tax-free.

For individuals dying in 1982, the federal government permits $225,000 to be given away as gifts during one's lifetime *or* at death without paying estate or gift taxes. This means that in 1982, estates of less than $225,000 are not subject to the federal estate and gift tax. The exclusion from the unified tax increases to $275,000 in 1983, $325,000 in 1984, $400,000 in 1985, $500,000 in 1986 and $600,000 in 1987 and thereafter.

NOTE: Despite the liberalized provisions of the new tax law, flower bonds still may have advantages for estates on which large estate taxes are due (see page 69).

Gifts and Bequests to Spouses

After January 1, 1982, there is no limit on the amount a married person may give or leave a spouse tax-free.

EXAMPLE: If, in 1982, Margaret left her entire $300,000 to her *husband,* there would be no federal estate tax due. If her *children* were the beneficiaries of her estate, $75,000 ($300,000 less the $225,000 exclusion) would be taxed.

Tax-Free Lifetime Gifts

Annual Exclusion

Since January 1, 1982, tax-free gifts of $10,000 or less may be made each year to an unlimited number of people.*

EXAMPLE: In 1982, Dorothy gives $10,000 to her daughter, $8,000 to her granddaughter, and $5,000 to a retiring employee on his 65th birthday. In 1983, Dorothy give another $10,000 to her daughter and $8,000 to her granddaughter. Dorothy pays no gift taxes on these gifts because none is more than $10,000.

* The tax-free limit had been $3,000 before passage of the 1981 Tax Act.

Annual exclusion gifts are separate from the gifts greater than $10,000 that are included in assets subject to the Unified Estate and Gift Tax.

EXAMPLE: If Dorothy gives $12,000 to her daughter in one year, $2,000 would be subject to the unified tax when Dorothy dies.

The annual exclusion is doubled to $20,000 for married couples even if only one spouse has income or assets, so long as the other spouse consents to the gift.

Charitable Gifts

There is no gift tax on outright charitable gifts of any amount.

Use of Trusts in Estate Planning

A *trust* is a legal arrangement under which one individual (the "grantor," "creator" or "settlor" of the trust) transfers ownership of his or her assets to a *trustee* (another individual or an institution) who manages the assets for the benefit of one or more *beneficiaries.*

Trusts are set up to control the disposition and use of assets and/or to minimize taxes.

Most Common Kinds of Trusts

Living (Inter Vivos) Trust
Created during one's lifetime; trust income received by the settlor or other beneficiaries.

A living trust is revocable. It may be terminated or changed during the settlor's lifetime. After the settlor's death, the trust becomes irrevocable. It then is administered for the benefit of beneficiaries according to the terms of the trust instrument (deed of trust).

Assets in a revocable trust are considered part of a decedent's estate and are subject to federal estate taxes, as they can be "taken back" by the settlor at any time.

If the trust is irrevocable—the settlor gives up the right to change or terminate the trust—and if the settlor does not receive income from the trust, the assets are not part of his or her estate, but are taxed as a gift at the time assets are transferred to the trust.

Trust Under Will (Testamentary)

The terms of a trust are stipulated in a will and are activated by the creator's, or testator's, death.

Irrevocable Insurance Trust

Vehicle for excluding proceeds of insurance policies from an estate and from estate taxes.

A funded insurance trust contains insurance policies and other assets. The trustee administers the trust and pays policy premiums during the settlor's lifetime.

An unfunded insurance trust is the owner and beneficiary of insurance on the life of the settlor, and is activated upon the settlor's death.

Marital and Residuary Trusts

Before the passage of the 1981 Tax Act, the use of a marital trust and a residuary or nonmarital trust was recommended frequently by estate planners to minimize estate taxes for marriages in which most of the assets are owned by one spouse.

Since January 1, 1982, no transfer of assets between spouses is taxable, and the amount of tax-free assets that may be given or bequeathed to anyone else increases from $225,000 in 1982 to $600,000 in 1987. This means there is less reason for married couple to use marital and residuary trusts for *tax savings.* However, trusts still can be used by individuals who want to assure that their assets go to their children or other beneficiaries after a spouse's death.

The Way the "New" Residuary Trust Might Work*

Upon Robert's death, the trust receives, at most, assets equal to the tax-free limit on gifts and inheritances ($225,000 in 1982, etc.). Judith, his wife, receives the balance of his assets as a direct, tax-free bequest.

The trust instrument (deed of trust) can be written so that Judith receives all the income earned by the trust during her lifetime. After her death, the assets in the trust pass tax-free to their children or other beneficiaries named by Robert.

---

* In family estate planning, it usually is assumed, and usually is true, that most of a couple's assets are owned by the husband. It is assumed also that the husband will die first.

Judith may leave the assets she inherited outright to whomever she wishes at her death, at which time the assets could be subject to federal estate taxes as part of her estate.

NOTE: If Judith has substantial assets, she might choose to make tax-free gifts (each year) to her children or other beneficiaries to reduce her taxable estate.

Whom to Name As Trustee

As with estate executors, individuals and institutions named as trustees should be selected because they are experienced, competent and trustworthy.

One of the advantages of naming a corporate trustee (a bank trust department or a nonbank trust company) is that institutions specialize in the organization and administration of trusts and estates. They employ investment managers, investment analysts, trust administrators, fiduciary law specialists and tax specialists whose efforts are coordinated for the benefit of the trustee's clients. An individual trustee might die or become incapacitated, but a corporate trustee is immune to the vagaries of human mortality. And although the best trust administrators are sensitive to the needs and wishes of their clients, they remain unbiased and independent from the entreaties and rivalries of family members.

Also, an institutional trustee is likely to have larger financial resources than an individual trustee, and, therefore, to be in a better position to make restitution in cases of fraud or mismanagement.

Most banks or trust companies will serve as "co-trustee" with a relative and/or valued personal adviser of the settlor. The reluctance of a settlor to appoint a corporate trustee for a trust that becomes effective after his or her death might be overcome by stipulating in the trust agreement that the individual trustee (e.g., the spouse) has the right to remove the corporate trustee and name another in its place. Or, the settlor might set up an *inter vivos* revocable trust which provides the opportunity to judge the trustee's competency during the settlor's lifetime.

Joint Ownership Between
Parents and Children

Joint ownerships are convenient as a means of access to assets, especially bank accounts, and as a means of transferring property quickly and easily when one of the joint owners dies. But joint ownerships between parents and children can create more problems than they solve.

The Case of the Adult Child and Elderly Parent

Mrs. Atkinson, a 70-year-old widow, has her 45-year-old daughter, Mary Ann, listed as joint owner on her NOW account. She wants Mary Ann to be able to draw on the account if Mrs. Atkinson becomes ill or otherwise unable to get to the bank. She also wants Mary Ann, her only child, to inherit the account when she dies, having heard that the automatic transfer of property reduces probate costs.

However, Mary Ann, who is in a much higher tax bracket than her mother, must pay an income tax on "her" share of the interest earned by the account. And, if Mary Ann dies before Mrs. Atkinson, the account could be taxed as part of Mary Ann's estate.

A preferable alternative: Mrs. Atkinson gives Mary Ann a power of attorney, an authorization for Mary Ann to act on her mother's behalf in all financial matters if Mrs. Atkinson becomes incompetent or incapacitated, and Mrs. Atkinson writes a simple will leaving all her assets to her daughter.

The Case of a Parent and Minor Child

Elizabeth, age 12, has received a $5,000 savings certificate from her grandparents. The certificate is registered "Jane Andrews, Custodian for Elizabeth Andrews, Uniform Gifts to Minors Act (State of Residence)." Legally, Elizabeth owns the certificate, but she will not have access to the funds until she reaches the age of majority (18 years old in some states, 21 in others).

If the certificate were registered in joint name, "Jane Andrews and Elizabeth Andrews," Elizabeth's mother Jane would have to pay taxes on "her" share of the interst earned by the certificate. If Mrs. Andrews should die, the certificate would become part of her taxable estate.

Where Things Are

After the trauma of losing a loved one, the task of tracking down the location of a will, bank accounts, insurance policies, etc. can be an emotionally draining and often frustrating experience for family members.

List the location of all documents and evidence of ownership of assets that might be needed by surviving family members and estate executors. Keep a copy of this list in a bedside or desk drawer. Let someone know it exists.

	LOCATION	ACCOUNT NUMBER
Will		
Life insurance policies		
Bank accounts		
Credit cards		
Security certificates		
Real estate deeds		
Rental leases		
Unpaid bills		
Notes on outstanding loans		
Notes receivable		
Automobile titles		
Other _____		
Safe deposit boxes		
Safe deposit box keys		

Getting Yours

For married couples, the question of how an asset should be owned—by the wife alone, by the husband alone, or by husband and wife together—arises in two important aspects of financial decision-making:

Who controls the asset; that is, who has the right to use it, sell it or give it away.

The *tax* advantages or disadvantages associated with "sole" or "joint" ownership.

There are several different kinds of legal ownership:

Sole Ownership
One person owns the property and may give it or sell it to whomever he or she wants.

Tenancy by the Entirety
A form of joint ownership between spouses. Each has an interest in the entire property. Neither spouse may dispose of the jointly owned asset without the other's consent. At the death of one spouse, the asset automatically becomes the property of the surviving spouse.

Joint Ownership with Rights of Survivorship
Also referred to as a joint tenancy. Each owner or "tenant" owns a half-interest in the property which may be sold or given to a third party while the original owners are living. At the death of one owner, the asset automatically becomes the property of the surviving owner.

Tenancy in Common

Each owner or "tenant" owns a half interest in the property which may be sold or given to a third party during the lifetimes of the joint owners. A tenancy in common differs from a joint tenancy in the respect that when a joint owner dies, his or her share passes to his or her heirs.

Community Property

In eight states—Arizona, California, Idaho, Louisiana, Nevada, New Mexico, Texas and Washington—all income and assets acquired while living in one of those states as a married couple are owned 50-50 as community property. Assets which are inherited, acquired before the marriage, or acquired in a noncommunity property state, may be separate property. Each spouse may bequeath his or her share of the community property to whomever he or she wishes; there are no rights of survivorship with community property.

Why Every Married Woman Should Have Assets in Her Own Name

On page 45, we discussed why a married woman should establish her own financial identity: to be prepared for the possibility of divorce or widowhood, to learn by doing, to have the satisfaction of being in control of her own financial well-being.

Having assets of her own not only is one way a woman can establish her own financial identity. It also can be crucial to her financial security.

This is not to say that *all* assets a couple owns jointly must be divided 50-50. It can be convenient for both spouses to have access to a joint checking account. It can save time and, possibly, money for jointly owned assets to become automatically and immediately the possessions of a surviving spouse. And some assets, such as a house, are neither practically nor easily divisible.

But there are other assets, such as savings instruments, securities, investment real estate properties and cars, that can be owned solely by either spouse. For example, if a couple purchases 200 shares of common stock, 100 shares can be registered in each name alone as easily as registering 200 shares in joint name.

The advantages of having assets in one's name alone become apparent—and necessary—when a marriage breaks up. A woman dependent on her husband for most or all of her financial support has no guarantee of financial security if assets are held in joint name or the assets are in his name alone. She is totally dependent on his good will to liquidate joint assets that will provide her with the means to support herself. Frequently, she must hire a lawyer and engage in protracted, expensive litigation until she receives her rightful share of the joint assets.

And, sadly, we hear too often of older women with poor prospects for training or employment who are left by their husbands and do not receive the assets they would have inherited had they remained married.

Even happily married women should have assets of their own so that they can share them with whomever they wish during their lifetimes and leave them to whomever they wish when they die. There is no assurance that even the most devoted husband will look after his wife's mother or any other people his wife cares about after she's gone.

Antenuptial Agreements

It has been said that the first time around you have bridesmaids and ushers; the second time, bankers and lawyers.

Any woman entering into a second marriage, especially if there are children from the first marriage, no matter how modest her means, should have an antenuptial agreement with her new spouse.

An antenuptial, or prenuptial, agreement is a legal contract written before a marriage takes place. The agreement usually is prepared by a lawyer. It describes the financial arrangements agreed to by the prospective spouses while they are married and the distribution of assets after their death or divorce.

The agreement provides the legal clarification of who owns what and to whom it goes in case of death or divorce. But an antenuptial agreement also can eliminate resentment and misunderstandings between spouses and among parents and children by dealing with a delicate situation realistically and fairly.

In some states, a husband or wife has the legal right to a specific share of a deceased spouse's estate if less than that share of the decedent's solely owned property is left to the surviving spouse. An antenuptial agreement can include a clause in which one or both spouses give up their *dower rights,* which is the right to *elect against the will,* or claim one's legal share of an estate.

On the other hand, there can be a provision in a will or antenuptial agreement that a spouse's estate will contribute to the financial support of a surviving spouse, should the need arise.

The Tax Man Cometh

No financial decision should be made solely on the basis of tax considerations, but every legitimate opportunity to eliminate, minimize or defer taxes should be explored.

Tax planning means thinking ahead. Tax planning should not be saved for tax preparation season. It should be done all year every year. It should be a part of the overall and continuous financial planning we discuss in the next and final section of the workbook.

Keeping Up with Changes in the Tax Laws

Income tax rules and regulations seem to change as often as the seasons. In many cases, the new laws affect financial decisions that must be made before the end of a calendar year. Major tax reforms, such as the 1981 Tax Act, are front-page news in most newspapers, and are covered extensively by specialized financial publications. When you see an item that seems to affect you, call your accountant or the local Internal Revenue Service (IRS) office for clarification. Also, buy an income tax guide, such as Sylvia Porter's *Income Tax Guide,* the *J. K. Lasser Tax Institute Guide,* the Prentice-Hall *Federal Tax Handbook,* or "Your Federal Income Tax for Individuals," available from the U.S. Treasury Department or the IRS. These publications analyze the current federal tax return line by line.

Consulting the Experts

Meet with your accountant several times a year to discuss your needs and objectives. Don't expect to do deliberative tax planning on

April 1 when you and the accountant are under pressure to meet the deadline for filing that year's return by April 15.

Not all accountants are equally competent tax advisers. If your accountant's ability is limited to converting tax records into tax returns once a year and you feel a need for professional guidance, find another accountant. The fee you pay for good tax planning, like the fee for tax return preparation, is a tax deductible expense. It can be more than offset by the money you get to keep in your pocket and out of Uncle Sam's.

Keeping Good Records

Have a ledger to record all sources of personal income and expenditures (if you have a business, keep separate records).

Keep all receipts for purchases and payments with tax consequences in a file, divided topically (e.g., Medicine and Drugs; Charitable Contributions; Moving Expenses). Make complete notations in your checkbook for all deposits and payments.

	DATE	DEPOSITS	
			ORDER OF _____ 19___

At the beginning of the year, label a large manila envelope "Taxes 19—." Use it for storing W-2 forms, "1099s" (confirmations of dividends and interest paid by banks and corporations), tax returns, the IRS instruction manual and any other tax-related materials that arrive in the mail.

Gross income
    Less: adjustments to income
    Equals:
Adjusted gross income (AGI)
    Less: itemized deductions and credits
    Equals:
Taxable income

The federal income tax is a *progressive* tax. Theoretically, this means the higher your income, the larger percentage of your income you pay in taxes. Until December 31, 1981, the highest tax rate on *earned* income (income from wages and salaries; also referred to as personal service income) is 50%, while the highest tax rate on *unearned* income (interest, dividends, rent, etc.) is 70%. Since January 1, 1982, the highest tax rate on income from any source is 50%. This is a *marginal* rate; that is, the highest rate paid on that *share* of your income that put you in the highest tax bracket.

You can cut your federal tax bill by taking advantage of the following exemptions, deductions and credits.

Take out your 1980 tax return. Go through it line by line to see if there are additional savings you can make for 1981, taking into account tax law changes that will apply to the 1982 tax return.

All line references are to 1981 Form 1040, used by individuals to itemize deductions.

Page references are to this workbook.

Filing Status

If you are married, should you file a joint return or separate returns?—Lines 2 and 3. (Also see "The Marriage Tax," page 144).

Are you an unmarried woman who qualifies for head of household status? Line 4.

* If you do not itemize deductions, use Form 1040A.

Exemptions

Have you taken exemptions for all your dependents? Lines 6a–6c.

Gross Income

Interest and dividend income—Lines 8a–8c. Interest income from municipal bonds (page 69) is exempt from federal income tax. For 1981 returns, $200 ($400 for joint returns) of other interest and dividend income is tax-free. Between 1982 and 1985, there will be a $100 ($200 on joint returns) exclusion on dividend income, but no exclusion for interest income. After 1985, 15% of interest income, with a maximum of $3,000, will be tax-free (15%, with a maximum of $6,000, on joint returns).

There is a *lifetime* exemption of $1,000 interest ($2,000 on joint returns) earned on All-Savers savings certificates (page 35). If the full exemption is taken in 1981, the income paid on All-Savers certificates in later years is taxable.

Are you entitled to a state or local income tax refund? Line 9.

Alimony—Line 10. Could your taxable alimony payments be changed to nontaxable child support?

Business income or loss—Line 11. If you have your own business, even if you work part-time at home, have you itemized deductible expenses such as advertising, telephone, postage and office supplies?

Capital gain or loss—Line 12 (see "Capital Gains and Losses," pages 141–143).

Pensions and annuities—Lines 15 and 16. Have you taken, or can you take, a tax-free distribution option on your pension or annuity (pages 106 and 114)?

Rents, royalties, partnerships, estates, trusts, etc.—Line 18. Have you deducted depreciation and other expenses from rental or royalty income (page 82)? Depletion allowances from royalties on gas and oil production (page 99)?

Adjustments to Income

Have you deducted moving expenses associated with your employment? Line 22.

Have you deducted business expenses for which you were not reimbursed by your employer? Line 23.

Have you taken the maximum allowable IRA contribution this year? Line 24 (see page 110).

Have you taken the maximum allowable contribution to a Keogh plan this year? Line 25 (see page 113).

Have you deducted the interest penalty (interest foregone) on early withdrawal from a savings certificate? Line 26 (see page 35).

Have you deducted alimony payments to a former husband? Line 27.

Do you qualify for the *disability income* exclusion? Line 28 (see pages 56–57).

Coming in 1982: U.S. citizens working abroad are permitted to exempt up to $75,000 of their income earned abroad from federal taxes. The exemption increases $5,000 a year to a maximum of $95,000 in 1986. Tax relief for two-income couples: The 1982 tax return will permit a deduction of 5% of the income of the lower-earning spouse, with a maximum deduction of $1,500. The deduction increases to 10%, and maximum to $3,000, in 1983.

Itemized Deductions

Medical and dental expenses

Medical insurance premiums; medicine and drugs; fees for professional health care services; transportation to and from medical treatment; hearing aids, dentures, eyeglasses, etc. line 32b.

Taxes

State and local income taxes

Real estate taxes

Sales taxes (use sales tax table or itemize for large purchases, such as a car)

Personal property taxes

Interest expense

Home mortgage

Mortgages on investment real estate

Bank loans

Credit card finance charges

Insurance policy loans

Other loans

Charitable contributions

Cash contributions for which you have receipts or cancelled checks

Other cash contributions

Noncash contributions (gifts of securities, works of art, clothing, other tangible goods; expenditures incurred as a volunteer, etc.)

Other deductible expenses (list incomplete)

Noninsured casualty or theft losses

Union dues

Political contributions

Dues to professional associations

Professional publication subscriptions

Employment agency fees

Tuition expenses to maintain or improve skills in current area of employment

Expenses associated with the production or collection of income (e.g., investment advisory fees, safe deposit box rental, purchase of The Money Workbook for Women).

Adjustments to income (Lines 22–30) and itemized deductions (Line 26) reduce taxable income. Credits (Lines 38–46) reduce the amount of tax you must pay.

Credits

Credit for contributions to candidates for public office—Line 38.

Credit for the elderly (individual or spouse 65 or over)—Line 39.

Credit for expenses associated with caring for children or other dependents—Line 40.

Investment credit for purchase of assets used in business or the production of income—Line 41.

Credit for payment of foreign income taxes—Line 42.

Credit to employers for hiring employees under a work incentive (WIN) program—Line 43.

Jobs credit to businesses which create new employment opportunities—Line 44.

Credit for installation of energy-saving devices—Line 45.

Do you qualify for the earned income credit—(Line 57)?

If your adjusted gross income (AGI) is less than $10,000 *and* you have a child who is (1) less than 19 years old, (2) a full-time student or (3) disabled, you might qualify. You receive a credit of 10% if your

AGI is less than $5,000, and a proportionately smaller credit as AGI approaches $10,000.

Adjusted gross income—itemized deductions and credits = taxable income.

NOTE: If, as you review your completely 1981 tax return, you discover adjustments, deductions or credits you might have taken but didn't, request a Form 1040X from your local IRS office. File it and get a tax refund. Better late than never!

Income Averaging

What It Is

Income averaging is an opportunity to lower your taxes in an unusually high income year by "spreading" the income over the current year and four previous years. The taxes on averaged income can add up to *less* than the total of taxes paid each year the income was earned.

How it Works

Your income in the high income year must be $3,000 more than 120% of your average gross income during the previous four years.

If you had a year of unusually high income within the past three years and did not "income average," you may do so now and file for a refund.

Income from dividends, interest, rent, royalties, capital gains, inheritances and gambling winnings qualify for income averaging, as well as earned income.

Capital Gains and Losses

A *capital gain* is the increase in value of a real or financial asset. If you paid $200 for a painting in 1976 and sold it this year for $400, your capital gain is $200. If you've got 100 shares of stock worth $5,000 for which you paid $3,000, you've got a $2,000 capital gain.

A capital loss is a decrease in value, the opposite of a capital gain.

Capital Gains

Taxes must be paid on capital gains, but only when an appreciated asset is sold. At that time, you have a realized gain. If appreciated assets are not sold, you have unrealized or "paper" gains.

To encourage investment in assets with potential for capital appreciation, the federal government taxes gains on assets owned at least one year and a day at a lower rate than it does ordinary income (income from all other sources, including short-term capital gains on assets owned for less than one year). You pay taxes on only 40% of a long-term capital gain.

> EXAMPLE: Virginia bought 100 shares of common stock in the American Energy Corporation for $10 a share, or $1,000, on October 5, 1981. She sold her shares for $12 a share, or $1,200, on October 6, 1982. Assuming she is in the 35% tax bracket, her after-tax return on a $1,000 investment is computed as follows:

Capital gain	$200	(difference between $1,200 and $1,000)
less	120	(60% of $200 gain not taxable)
Taxable capital gain	$ 80	
Capital gains tax (35% of $80)	$ 28	
After-tax return ($200 − $28)	$172	
Percentage return on $1,000	17.2%	
Actual tax rate	14%	($28 is 14% of $200)

Capital Gains on House Sales

If you sell your house for more than you paid for it, you do not have to pay a capital gains tax if, within two years, you use the sales proceeds to buy a new residence. If you do not buy another house, and you are less than 55 years old, you must pay a capital gains tax on any appreciated value. However, the cost of capital improvements made over the years you owned your home (e.g., a new roof, electrical wiring, conversion of a garage to a den) may be added to the price you paid for the house to give you a lower net gain.

If you are 55 years old or older, sell a house you've lived in for at least three of the past five years, and do not buy a new house, you may take a tax-free capital gain of up to $125,000. This exemption may be taken only one time by each taxpayer. Married couples who own their home jointly are considered to be one taxpayer for the residential capital gains tax exclusion. Only one spouse need be 55 years old to qualify.

Capital Losses

Just as the value of an asset can go up, it can go down. If it does, you've got a capital loss.

The only good thing that can be said about a capital loss is that it can be used to lower your taxes. A capital loss may be subtracted from capital gains or other taxable income earned in the same year the loss is incurred, or carried forward to future years until you die.

Long-term and short-term capital losses have different tax consequences. One dollar of a loss taken on an asset owned for one year or less (a short-term loss) may be used to offset one dollar of capital gain or ordinary income. It takes two dollars of a long-term loss (a loss on an asset owned more than one year) to offset one dollar of capital gains or ordinary income.

The maximum taxable income that may be reduced in one year by short-term or long-term losses is $3,000. However, short-term losses greater than $3,000 and long-term losses greater than $6,000 may be "carried forward" and used in future years to offset capital gains and other taxable income.

Estimating the Coming Year's Taxes

If your income comes in irregular flows, or from sources not subject to an employer's withholding, then every three months you must file an estimated quarterly tax return with the Internal Revenue Service, and, if necessary, with the state.

The estimate is based on your *expectation* of the *amount* of income you will receive and *when* you will receive it. If less than 80% of the taxes due are paid before the end of the year in which the income is earned, IRS will charge a penalty for "under-withholding."*

You are not required to pay estimated taxes if you expect one of the following:

1. Your unearned income (interest, dividends, rent, etc.) to be less than $500.

2. Your earned income to be less than $20,000 and you are unmarried, a head of household, a surviving spouse, or married to a nonworking spouse.

3. Your earned income to be less than $10,000 between you and your employed spouse.

4. Your tax payments to be less than $100.

Estimated quarterly tax payments are due on the 15th day of April, June, September and January.

Forms for filing estimated taxes are available at local IRS offices and state revenue agencies.

The Marriage Tax

The 1981 Tax Act brings some relief from the punitive "marriage tax," but not enough to satisfy the two-paycheck families it penalizes. As it is and will continue, families with two wage earners pay a higher tax on their combined incomes than they would if they were single and filing two separate returns.

For example, two unmarried taxpayers earning $15,000 a year each would have paid about $2,500 in federal taxes last April. A married couple with the same income would have owed Uncle Sam almost $6,000, an unholy matrimonial penalty of 20%.

The progressive income tax is based on a social philosophy that says the more you earn, the larger the burden you should carry of the cost of public services. But current tax law also is based on the assumption that all income in a family is pooled and allocated by joint decision.

---

* There is no penalty if the amount of taxes paid equals the previous year's taxes, even if the current year's income and tax obligation are higher.

This assumption no longer is as valid as it once might have been. Many working couples share basic household expenses, but spend or save the residual of their incomes as each pleases or must. This often includes an obligation to support ex-wives or children from a previous marriage, a burden most second spouses neither want nor can afford to share.

In Washington, they say tax reform is a complicated matter, and that the interests of many competing groups must be balanced to arrive at an equitable distribution of income and taxes. With 24 million married women in the labor force, one would think that they and their husbands are a significant part of the U.S. population whose perception of equity should not be overlooked.

It's easy enough to get rid of the marriage tax: Just let married people have the option of filing as single taxpayers.

If you agree, write to:

The Honorable Dan Rostenkowski III
Chairman of the Committee on Ways & Means
House of Representatives
1102 Longworth House Office Building
Washington, D.C. 20515

Will Your Tax Return Be Audited?

An *audit* is a review of your tax return by an agent employed by the Internal Revenue Service. According to *All You Need to Know About the IRS,* by Paul Strassels and Robert Wool, the purpose of tax audits is *to keep taxpayers honest through the fear of being caught doing something dishonest.**

---

* *All You Need to Know About the IRS* is an informative and easy-to-read guide to tax planning, as well as an unusually candid exposition of the workings and mentality of IRS agents.

How Tax Returns Are Selected for Audit

Every tax return received by IRS is put into the IRS computer. A number of taxpayers in each income bracket is selected at random by the computer for audit. Other returns send up a "red flag" to the computer indicating something out of line for "average" or "normal" deductions in the taxpayer's income bracket, occupational category or geographic area.

About 2% of all individual (e.g., nonbusiness) tax returns are audited each year. The chances of being audited increase as your income increases. Among 1979 tax returns of taxpayers who itemized deductions, 2.25% in the $10,000 to $15,000 adjusted gross income (AGI) bracket were audited, 2.91% in the $15,000 to $50,000 bracket, and 10.55% with incomes of $50,000 or more.*

Audits can be made up to six years following the year in which a return is filed. Generally, only returns for the immediate past three years are audited. However, all cancelled checks, bank statements and other tax records should be kept for at least six years. There is no time limit on the IRS's right to audit fraudulent returns.

An audit can begin and end with a brief review, of which you are unaware, by an IRS agent at his or her desk, or it can attract excessive scrutiny and require your participation.

What to Do if You Are Called for an Audit

You will receive written notification of the time and date of an interview with an IRS agent and a request for information relating to specific items on your tax return.

If you have reported all *taxable* income and *legitimate* deductions, you have nothing to fear from an audit.

You may go to the audit alone or with your spouse. Your accountant or lawyer may accompany you or go in your place as your authorized representative.

You decide whether to hold the audit at the IRS office, your home, your office or your accountant's or lawyer's office.

Be prepared to justify with written documentation the specific items in question. This might include the worksheets you used to prepare your tax return, bank statements and cancelled checks,

* Strassels and Wool, page 75.

bank deposit slips, confirmations of dividends and interest, confirmations of security purchases and sales, expense account records, your business appointment calendar, receipts for cash expenses, and receipts for cash or nonmonetary charitable contributions.

Answer questions politely and precisely. Do not volunteer information for which you are not asked.

If the auditor concludes that you have underpaid (e.g., the agent disallows a contribution of old clothes to the Salvation Army or some business entertainment expenses you've deducted), and you or your accountant believe the deductions are justified, you may ask to speak with the auditor's supervisor. If this brings no satisfaction, you may appeal the auditor's decision to the IRS's Appellate Division and, after that, to federal Tax Court.

15

Nobody Looks Out for Your Interests as Well as You Do Yourself: Financial Planning in Action

Financial planning is the most effective way to organize our financial lives. It provides a structure within which we can think ahead, set goals, and coordinate the financial decisions that will help us reach those goals.

We began the financial planning process in Section 1 by taking financial inventory (step one) and setting goals (step two).

Now you should be ready to move on to step three—developing a financial plan—and step four, implementing the plan.

Step Three—Developing a Financial Plan

On page 25, you listed your financial goals, the things that motivate you to work hard, save and invest. Perhaps you said you want to open the candy store you yearned for as a little girl, or have enough money some day to escape northern winters and bask in California sunshine. At this stage, we get to the nitty-gritty of how you turn those visions of bonbons and palm trees into a reality. Now is the time to figure out *how much* you will need and *when* you will need it.

Whether your goal is to accumulate a specific amount of money, such as $5,000 to start a business, or to have adequate income from investments, say $20,000, to support year-round jogs on the beach, the name of the game is *asset-building,* making your savings and investments grow over a period of years.

To develop a workable financial plan, you need to estimate *how much* you need to accumulate for each goal you set, and *when* you will need it. Of course, you will be making assumptions about future income, rates of inflation and rates of return on investments, but you will be operating within the framework of a well-thought-out, coordinated plan.

Begin by filling in a worksheet (below) for each goal you set for yourself on page 25 (*except retirement planning*), using the Accumulation Table (page 131) to determine the amount of funds you need to accumulate each year until you reach your goal. Use the worksheets on pages 113–114 for retirement planning. Remember to include the last line on page 114—how much you must accumulate each year for your retirement goal—in the total amount on page 179 you must accumulate each year to reach all your goals on page 15.

> **REMEMBER:** Long-term accumulation comes *after* you've set aside your savings nest egg (Section 2) and provided for adequate insurance (Section 4).

How Much Will You Need to Save or Invest Each Year to Have the Lump Sum Accumulated to Reach the Goal You've Set?

---

1. Describe your goal   _____
2. Financial goal   _____   *

                                           _____   †

                                           _____

3. Deduct currently owned assets already committed to this goal   _____
4. Additional amount to be accumulated   _____

    Turn to accumulation table (page 118)

5. Find the *row* that corresponds to the rate of interest you think you could earn each year during the accumulation period.   ___ %

---

* Pre-tax accumulation.
† Use additional lines for financial goals with staggered time horizons, such as the four years you would pay college tuitions.

6. Find the *column* of years that corresponds to the number of years until you reach your goal. ___years

7. Divide the additional amount you need to accumulate during those years by the amount at the *intersection* of the above row and column and multiply by $1,000. $ _____

$ _____

8. This is how much you need to set aside each year to accumulate the lump sum on Line (1). $ _____

How Much Will You Need to Put Aside Each Year to Reach Your Goals?

Total the amounts on Line 8 on each worksheet and on the last line of page 105 for retirement planning. Because different goals have different time horizons, you will need to accumulate more during some years than others.

YEAR	ACCUMULATION GOAL	YEAR	ACCUMULATION GOAL
1.	_____	21.	_____
2.	_____	22.	_____
3.	_____	23.	_____
4.	_____	24.	_____
5.	_____	25.	_____
6.	_____	26.	_____
7.	_____	27.	_____
8.	_____	28.	_____
9.	_____	29.	_____
10.	_____	30.	_____
11.	_____	31.	_____
12.	_____	32.	_____
13.	_____	33.	_____
14.	_____	34.	_____
15.	_____	35.	_____
16.	_____	36.	_____
17.	_____	37.	_____
18.	_____	38.	_____
19.	_____	39.	_____
20.	_____	40.	_____

Where Will the Money Come from?

The funds to reach your goals will come primarily from three sources:

Surplus income (what's left over after paying for living expenses)

Currently owned assets

Inheritances

Do you think your surplus income through the years, currently owned assets and inheritances will provide the funds you need to reach your goals?

If not, what can you do to increase your income? Cut back on expenses? (Refer to Personal Income Statement, page 28.)

If not, are you willing to assume the additional risk needed to increase the income you earn on your investments? (See "The Risk-Return Trade-Off, page 60.)

If not, you must scale down your financial goals to the point at which they are realistic and attainable.

Step Four—Implementing Your Financial Plan

This is the time to choose the savings instruments, insurance coverage and investments that make your financial plan a reality. This is when you decide whether you want to invest in stocks, bonds or real estate to reach your retirement goal. Do you want to keep your savings nest egg in a money market fund or savings certificates? Does whole life or term insurance provide the best coverage for your family?

Fill in the worksheet on page 153 titled My (Our) Financial Plan. Savings and insurance are already listed, as they should be everyone's top priority. Fill in your remaining financial goals in order of their importance to you.

My (Our) Financial Plan

_____
(date)

FINANCIAL GOAL	VEHICLES	CURRENT AMOUNTS	TARGET AMOUNT YEAR 1	TARGET AMOUNT YEAR 2	TARGET AMOUNT YEAR 3
Savings					
Insurance					
Life Insurance					
Disability					
Health					
Homeowners'					
Automobile					
Personal Liability					

Where Do You
Go for Help? (See chart, pages 140, 141)

At some point you'll be seeking professional assistance: for information, for advice, or for following through on the different aspects of your Financial Plan.

The chart on pages 156 and 157 is a general directory of the different financial institutions or individuals who offer the financial products and services you might want.

How to Choose a Financial Adviser

Throughout this workbook, we have stressed the importance of being well-informed and having control over one's financial life. But there is a limit to what even the best-informed and most efficient woman can do for herself. This is why we seek out professional advisers, individuals who have the experience and expertise to point out the different options we might pursue and the facilities to implement the decisions we make.

Ideally, a financial adviser has proficiency and is able to assist in all aspects of a client's financial affairs. There is a small but growing group of financial professionals called financial planners who take this coordinated approach. Most financial professionals continue to specialize—in investments, accounting, law, insurance, etc.—and for the most part serve their clients within their areas of expertise.

How do you find a competent financial adviser? The best way is through a personal referral. Ask for recommendations from someone whose opinion you value. If that is not possible, pick several names with addresses convenient to your home or office from the telephone directory (This potluck method is as likely to produce satisfactory results as calling the office of a national professional association, such as the American Bar Association).

You should not make a commitment to hand over your financial affairs to anyone until you sit down for at least an hour to get to know one another. This is the time to ask about professional credentials and experience, how much the service will cost, and for the names of several clients you may call for a reference. This is the time to decide whether you will feel comfortable working with the people you meet.

Do you like them? Do they inspire confidence? Seem to know what they're talking about? Make recommendations suitable for your particular situation and needs? Act as if you will be a valued customer?

Unfortunately for people of modest means, the services of a good financial adviser do not come cheap.* Most work for a fee at an hourly rate. Some advisers scale their fees according to the client's income. Others set a minimum fee, such as $1,000 or $2,000. However, because the fees for financial advisory services are considered "expenses associated with the production or collection of income," they are partly or wholly tax deductible.

You want to choose a financial adviser who works on a fee-paying basis rather than on commission because this is the best way to assure that the advice you are getting is objective advice. There are, for example, people calling themselves "financial planners" who sell a product, such as mutual funds or insurance. They tell prospective clients there is no charge for their advisory services, but too often the clients find that the best way to reach their goals is to buy the products the so-called planner sells and on which he or she earns a commission. It is not impossible, but it is much more difficult, to provide an objective analysis when your primary motivation is to sell something.

Whomever you choose, remember that it's *your* money and *your* well-being that's at stake. Do not continue to patronize an individual or organization if you think you're not getting the quality of service and advice you should receive. Don't be intimidated by the presence of a "busy, important expert." Don't be afraid to ask "dumb" questions or say "That doesn't sound quite right to me." Don't move on to a new topic until you feel confident you understand the subject being discussed.

We need and should use professionals for their experience and ability to implement our financial decisions, but remember: *Nobody looks out for your interests as well as you do yourself.*

---

* Perhaps one day financial professionals who are women will set up clinics and contribute their services at nominal rates to counsel women who otherwise could not afford them.

Where to Go for Help

FINANCIAL PRODUCT OR SERVICE	FINANCIAL INSTITUTIONS OR INDIVIDUALS								
	Commercial Bank	Thrift Institution	Money Market Fund	Insurance Agent	Stock & Bond Broker	Mutual Fund	Real Estate Broker	Silver & Gold Dealer	Investment Adviser
Savings Instruments	X	X	X						
Insurance				X					
Stocks, Bonds & Mutual Funds					X	X			X
Real Estate							X		
Silver & Gold	X							X	X
Collectibles									X
Tax Shelters					X				X
Retirement Planning	X	X			X	X			X
Estate Planning									
Tax Planning									

Where to Go for Help

FINANCIAL INSTITUTIONS OR INDIVIDUALS	FINANCIAL INSTITUTIONS OR INDIVIDUALS						
	Bank Trust Department	Collectibles Vendor	Tax Shelter Specialist	Lawyer	Accountant	Tax Lawyer	Financial Planner
Savings Instruments							X
Insurance							X
Stocks, Bonds & Mutual Funds	X						X
Real Estate							X
Silver & Gold							X
Collectibles		X					X
Tax Shelters			X	X	X	X	X
Retirement Planning	X						X
Estate Planning	X			X	X		X
Tax Planning					X	X	X

Step Five—Periodically Reviewing and Revising

A financial plan is like a road map. It helps you get to where you think you want to go. But after you've set up your plan, you might decide the road you chose originally is too narrow or bumpy. Perhaps you want to take a different route.

That's why step five of the planning process is important. You want to review your plan at least once a year, and revise it if the plan no longer meets your needs or measures up to your expectations.

You'll want to make changes as your personal situation changes. There might be more or less income than you'd anticipated. The dependent children you had might no longer be at home, or you might be closer to retirement age.

The savings instruments, investments or insurance policies you've chosen might not measure up to the expectations you had when you selected them. Cut your losses. Find another investment or another adviser, whatever you need to get back on track.

Things happen in our economy which affect your outlook and planning. A major change in the tax laws, such as the Tax Act of 1981, or a string of years with double-digit inflation, can affect the financial decisions you make now and will make in the future.

Financial planning is a lifelong process, and once you begin to plan, it becomes a way of life. But the planning process must never be thought of as an end in itself. *The sole purpose of planning is to provide for the financial security and well-being of ourselves and our families.*

Are you ready to begin?

Good luck!